Dried Flowers

Dried Flowers

DRYING & ARRANGING

SUSAN CONDER

Consultant: Hannah Stanley
Special Arrangements: Dee Hine

DAVID R. GODINE
Boston

In memory of Jeanne Hudes Levine

First U.S. edition published in 1988 by
David R. Godine, Publisher, Inc.
Horticultural Hall
300 Massachusetts Avenue
Boston, Massachusetts 02115

Originally published in the U.K. by
Merehurst Press, London

LC 87–45830
ISBN 0–87923–719–8

First U.S. edition

Edited by Joyce Becker
Designed by Roger Daniels
Arrangements photographed by Steve Lee, assisted by Ciff Morgan
Additional photography by Graham Tann
Typeset by Lineage, Watford, England
Colour Separation by Fotographics Ltd, London–Hong Kong
Printed in Italy

The Publishers would like to thank The Flowering Dutchman, dried flower wholesalers, of Unit 3, Hanover West Industrial Estate, 161 Acton Lane, London NW10 7NB for their advice and expertise.

The Publishers would like to thank the following for their help:
The Covent Garden General Store, 111 Long Acre, Covent Garden, London WC2

Multiflora, Covent Garden Market, Nine Elms Lane, London SW8

Silk flowers from a selection at Neal Street East, the Oriental specialist,
5 Neal Street, Covent Garden, London WC2

Valerie Groves and Nicholas Lodge, Fleurs du Monde, Bournemouth

Brenda Purton

Seija Basi

Daphne Vagg

Neville, Gabriel and Alexandra Conder

The Author would like to thank Hannah Stanley, Dee Hine, Steve Lee, Cliff Morgan and Joyce Becker for their help in producing this book.

Contents

In the last ten years dried flowers have thrown off the frowsy image they acquired in the early part of the century when grubby pampas grasses and dusty Chinese lanterns were dull leftovers from the Victorian era. For one thing, the range of dried plants now available is vastly more interesting and varied. Many are home-grown, others are imported from abroad, adding exotic flowers, seedheads and spathes to familiar favourites.

Techniques of drying and preserving have changed little over the centuries; the sand method that preserved the garlands in Tutankhamun's tomb is still used to dry flowers today. Silica gel and detergent powders may have added to the range of desiccants, and microwave ovens may have speeded up the process a little, but it is the manner of using these dried materials that has changed.

In an age of 'separates' and 'mix and match' to achieve greater variety in clothes and furnishings, this book applies the same versatility to dried flowers. There are suggestions for arranging them on their own, with fresh, preserved and evergreen foliage, with house plants, with fruits and cones, with figurines and with artificial flowers. There are styles for almost every situation and occasion, including Christmas and weddings, and in sizes from the very impressive to the tiniest of miniatures. And there are alternative suggestions for colour schemes and plant groupings with each idea.

If you ever thought that dried flowers were not for you, I believe this book will make you change your mind because the ideas are practical for today's decor and our busy lives.

DAPHNE VAGG
Editor of *The Flower Arranger*
Judge, teacher and demonstrator for The National Association of Flower
Arrangement Societies of Great Britain.

Dried Flowers

Flowers have been dried, for various reasons, for thousands of years. The ancient Egyptians made immensely detailed preparations for their dead to enjoy all that they had during this life in the next one, the existence of which was never in doubt. Preserved garlands of flowers were placed in their tombs.

Many centuries later, and for those living in this world to enjoy, medieval monks harvested and dried flowers and herbs for medicinal use. The method used – hanging bunches upside-down to dry – is virtually that used today. Later still, the seventeenth century Italian, Giovanni Batista Ferrari, gave instructions in his book *Flora – ouero Cultura di Fiori* for the drying of flowers by burying them in clean sand and removing them several months later.

The Victorians applied their usual frenzied industriousness and commitment to embellishing all things natural to dried flowers. Skills in floral handicraft were considered a necessary requisite for any well bred Victorian female, and it was even felt that from the structure of the flowers themselves moral lessons could be learned.

As well as displaying dried flowers in glass domes, dismembered dried flowers – and even dried seaweed – provided the raw material for velvet-backed pictures. Pine and other conifer cones were likewise dismembered, and the scales used, like overlapping fish scales, to make baskets. Upright stalks of lavender or barley were interwoven with green ribbon to make flower pot covers.

Today, dried flowers are very popular, although some people still consider them as second best to fresh flowers. The relationship between fresh and dried flowers is rather like that between fresh and dried apricots. The fresh and dried fruit are quite different, but equally delicious and useful.

The same is true for dried flowers, and their potential and beauty can only be fully appreciated when they are accepted within their own context. Even the most realistically preserved flower lacks the ephemeral quality of a fresh one, and it would be misleading to imply otherwise. A fresh flower, especially if scented, automatically has a 'fresh from the garden' charm, even if the particular garden is that of a commercial grower thousands

of miles away; and the flower has spent much intervening time in refrigerated transport and florist's cold store.

Once that essential difference between fresh and dried flowers is faced, and that particular demon exorcised, the virtues of dried flowers become apparent. Dried flowers, after all, are natural ones, with all the infinite and interesting variation in colour, form and size that is lacking in manufactured flowers. Dried flowers are long lasting, and therefore economical, and can be re-used several times. They are tolerant of most temperatures, whether created by central heating or summer sun. They offer a wide range of subtle and striking colours, and they do offer seasonal references. Preserved flowers, seed pods and foliage are especially useful in autumn and winter, and, depending upon the choice of material, can reflect the current garden scene or be reminiscent of spring and summer.

Although statice and immortelles or everlastings – ammobium, helichrysum, acroclinium, helipterum and xeranthemum – are fairly easily grown, sun-loving annuals, harvesting them at the peak of their beauty does rob the garden, especially if the garden is an ordinary size. If there is enough space, treat these flowers for drying like the crop that they are, and grow them in rows in the vegetable garden, where their absence won't be an eyesore. In any case, everlastings are easy to buy, and it would be more sensible to grow some of the rarer annuals for drying.

Celosia, or cockscomb, with its velvety, old-fashioned appeal, is a good choice; there are mixed seeds available with red, yellow, pink, salmon and gold flower heads. Bells of Ireland; annual scabious, or moon flower; love-in-a-mist; love-lies-bleeding; and zinnias – if you are prepared to preserve them in a desiccant – are other good choices.

There are seed mixtures available of annual flowers suitable for drying, including gomphrena and rhodanthe as well as the usual immortelles. Mixtures of ornamental grasses are also available. Perennial seed mixtures of plants for drying usually contain Chinese lantern, poppy, sea holly, *Iris foetidissima*, achillea, echinops, anaphalis, thrift, allium and sea lavender. It seems a less satisfactory idea than the annual mixture, though, as the plants' heights, spreads, cultivation needs and growth rates vary. A moderately strong echinops could swamp a clump of slow-growing thrift or iris in no time at all.

Whatever the choice of flowers, a good seed bed needs to be prepared, as some seeds do not germinate easily. Use very little fertilizer, or too much foliar growth will be made at the expense of flowers.

If space is limited, concentrate primarily on making a nice garden, with one proviso: use attractive plants suitable for drying or preserving, which are not so easily bought, and which continue to look attractive after harvesting. There are many shrubs with foliage that can be preserved in glycerine, and gentle pruning provides the raw material without denuding the garden. Among the most reliable are spotted laurel, beech, box, camellia, choisya, cotoneaster, elaeagnus, eucalyptus, fatsia, griselinia, ivy, evergreen shrubby honeysuckle, magnolia, mahonia, laurel, rhododendron and laurustinus. Broom can be air dried, as can eucalyptus and various artemisias.

Good, all round ground cover plants with foliage which can be treated include ferns; Corsican hellebore and stinking hellebore; pachysandra and Solomon's seal. You can, by discreet and self-controlled harvesting – one or two leaves, for example – have a pleasant garden and good dried material. Hosta leaves – always lovely in a garden unless the slugs gain control – can be air dried, and assume attractively twisted shapes. Preserved foliage is especially difficult to buy, and the raw material is quite easy to grow, even in the shadiest garden.

Seed pods of poppy, hypericum, paeony, some iris, mullein and allium are also good value, as the pleasure of the flowering period is not cut short. The flowers of popular dried pods such as Chinese lantern and honesty are insignificant, and their only garden value is in the pod stage.

Harvesting

There are a few general rules about harvesting. The many qualifying clauses are covered separately, plant by plant, in the chart on page 140. Always harvest on a dry day, as morning dew or rain clinging on the flowers and foliage can cause rot. To ensure best results, always harvest during a spell of warm, dry, sunny weather – a long wet spell results in turgid, soft plant growth, which is difficult to dry, and which will show excessive shrinkage.

Harvesting of some seed pods and the annual flowers that dry naturally in autumn can be tricky. In cool temperate climates, summers are often disappointing, and every last bit of sunlight is needed, but the first hard frost can turn the hoped-for crop into a useless, sodden, blackened pulp, and gale-force winds will produce only weather-beaten skeletons. Be aware of impending local frosts and avoid growing plants for drying in known frost pockets, areas exposed to high winds or to early morning mists.

Preserving inferior material is a waste of time. Any discoloration, tears or holes in the petals or foliage, become very obvious when dried or preserved. Obviously, one or two damaged leaves can be discreetly removed from an otherwise perfect branch before preserving.

Some plants can be picked at various stages in their development.

Wild grasses, for example, can be picked while in flower and yellow with pollen or when fully ripe and going gold. Dyer's greenwood can be picked when its fat buds are all green, or when they have opened to reveal bright orange centres. Teasel and burdock can be picked when green or when fully ripe and brown.

Many flowers, such as hollyhock and yellow loosestrife, have equally attractive flowers and seed pods. For flowers with one optimum moment for harvesting, it is usually just before the flowers are fully open and before the colour fades. Visible pollen or seeds, or wilting or missing lower florets on flower spikes, indicate an overmature flower. If it is the seed pod that is being collected, it should not show signs of splitting open. To prevent dropping, harvest fluffy material, such as clematis and pampas grass, when the seed pods are hairy but not yet fluffy. They continue to ripen and become fluffy as they dry; if harvested when fully ripe and fluffy, they fall apart. An aerosol fixative, such as hair spray, can help prevent very fragile and delicate seed heads shattering.

Foliage preserved with glycerine or antifreeze needs to be mature – mid- to late summer is usually the best time to collect it. Young green foliage will not absorb the solution adequately, and either wilts or shrivels. Autumn is usually too late, because the sap is no longer rising and natural senescence has started so the solution will not be drawn up through the stems. Leaves with autumn colouring have already stopped taking in sap, and so are unsuitable for glycerining, although they can be pressed between layers of newspaper. Evergreens take up antifreeze solution at a slower rate in winter, and tend to have new, soft growth in spring, so late summer is best for them, too.

Wild Plants

Collecting wild plants for drying, like collecting edible wild plants, has a small but devoted following. The irony is that, once preserved and presented in a domestic setting, wild flowers, foliage and seed pods take on a rarity value, rather like the wild mushrooms lavishly described on a restaurant menu.

Some plants are protected by law and no part – roots, flowers, seeds, stems or foliage – may be taken. Protected plants vary from place to place; local authorities can supply a list, and larger local libraries may also have this information. Permission must also be gained from the land owner of fields or woodlands before entering to search for suitable plants for preservation. This is not always easy to do, and taking common roadside or hedgerow materials is unlikely to cause any offence. Use a pair of secateurs when collecting, for a quick, clean cut. Pulling up plants is unnecessary and very destructive, and against all environmental preservation principles. The plants suggested below grow wild in most temperate climates, but equivalent plants can be found in other climates.

Among common wild plants particularly useful for their seed heads are cow parsley; teasel; rose-bay willowherb, or fireweed; various grasses; hops; polygonum; dock and sorrel; plantain; mullein; foxglove; rushes; sedges; thistles; burdock; clover; bulrushes, or cattails; meadowsweet and nipplewort. Buttercups; various mints; sneezewort; yarrow; wild chamomile; heather; knapweed; yellow loosestrife; purple loosestrife; feverfew and tansy are common and attractive wild flowers.

Because some time can elapse between collecting wild flowers and starting the drying process, place delicate specimens, which might wilt, in a plastic bag, then seal. Don't leave them in the bag indefinitely, or they may rot instead.

Ferns can be pressed between sheets of newspaper placed under the carpet, a pile of books or mattress, as can bracken, a lovely autumnal filler for dried arrangements. Wild rose hips, thorn haws and guelder rose berries can be preserved with glycerine, varnished or left as is, to very slowly wither.

Tree and shrub branches are indispensible for large-scale arrangements and, on a smaller scale, for adding personal touches to the florist's mixture of dried flowers. Obviously native trees vary from one locality to the next, but those with coloured bark, such as red-tinged dogwood or green-tinged spindle; an elegant habit of growth, such as hazel or birch; or attractive cones, such as alder, are good choices.

Preserving Flowers and Foliage

There are basically two ways to preserve plant material, although there are several different techniques for each method. Most plant preservation involves drying, either by exposing the material to a combination of air and heat, or by surrounding it with a desiccant, such as sand, alum or silica gel, which absorbs moisture from the plant cells. Some types of foliage are preserved by standing them in diluted glycerine or antifreeze, which is drawn up into the plant by osmosis and replaces the plant's own water content; thus preserving it.

Although there are tried and true techniques for preserving certain flowers – drying garden roses in a desiccant, for example – experimenting with different methods can produce interesting results. As no book could possibly include every plant worth drying, you may have to experiment.

Different techniques may be used on the same material for different effects. Eucalyptus leaves, for example, remain bluey grey, but brittle, when air dried; and remain pliable, taking on rich mahogany tones, when treated in glycerine. Some plants are best dried using one technique at one stage of growth, and a different technique at another. Hydrangeas in their full bloom should be dried with desiccant, while those already starting to dry naturally on the bush, towards the end of summer, need to be dried with their stems resting in a small amount of water. The charts on pages 140-143 include suggested treatment for each of the plants listed.

Preserving by air drying

Air drying is as simple as it sounds, and involves no special techniques or equipment. The drying period can range from a week to several months, depending on the type of material, when and where it was harvested, and the humidity of the place where it is drying. Dried flowers, however, tend to become rather brittle and those dried by being hung upside down can have unnaturally straight stems.

The most obvious choice is the everlasting flowers – members of the *Compositae* family, such as straw flowers, helipterums and xeranthemums, which originate in hot sunny climates and have paper-thin petals or petal-like bracts. These contain very little moisture and will often dry of their own accord in the garden.

Other suitable candidates include seed heads, such as honesty; the globe-shaped head of communal garden chives, onions and leeks; and the large, flat seed heads of members of the *Umbelliferae* family, such as cow parsley, or Queen Anne's lace, angelica and fennel. Large spiky seed heads include those of mullein and hollyhock. Grasses – both wild and ornamental – generally have much smaller seed heads but are also ideal for air drying.

Flowers with heads composed of many tiny blossoms, such as gypsophila, lady's mantle and achillea, are suitable, as are those whose beauty comes from petal-like bracts, such as acanthus; or leaf-like calyces, such as Chinese lantern or the woolly-grey *Helichrysum petiolatum.*

Technique

The goal is to dry the plant material as quickly as possible, because the longer it takes a flower to dry, the more colour is lost. Warmth, protection from direct sunlight (which fades the colour of some flowers), a dry atmosphere and plenty of ventilation are necessary. Bunches of flowers might look nice hanging up to dry in a kitchen, but the steamy atmosphere can be counterproductive.

Attics or dark corners of unused rooms are possibilities, provided there is an adequate circulation of air. Outbuildings, such as garages or sheds, are usually damp and without adequate ventilation. The space used should also be dust free.

If you are drying flowers, strip the leaves as soon as possible after picking, as they retain moisture and slow down the drying process. They are also easier to remove when fresh than when brittle and dry. Large flowers should be dried individually, and bunches of flowers should ideally contain one type only, as drying times vary. The bunches should be small enough to allow the air to circulate freely and loose enough not to entangle or crush the inner flowers.

Drying time depends on the type and moisture content of the material and the conditions in which it is drying. Drying time for a particular plant can vary from one year to the next, depending on the weather. Material that is fully dry should feel crisp and the stems should snap. Check the 'neck' of the stem, just under the flower, as this is usually the last place to dry out. Stand a sample upright for a day or two; if it is still moist, the flower head will droop.

Because stems tend to shrink as they dry, it is often necessary to re-tie bunches or individual flowers part-way through the drying process. Stout twine is traditional, tied round the stems twice, so it is self adjusting, then in a bow. Rubber bands are also self adjusting, but they need to be attached to wire for hanging. Plastic-coated wire, such as garden ties and freezer-bag ties, can also be used.

Suitable foliage for drying includes *Magnolia grandiflora*, silver artemisias, aspidistra and bamboos, which are actually giant grasses.

For drying flowers and foliage upside down, an old-fashioned wooden drying rail which can be raised and lowered by a pulley, is useful in a high-ceilinged room. Alternatives include cup hooks fixed to the underside of beams; coat hooks or nails fixed to walls; telescopic wall hung towel rails; ordinary clothes line; and the open trusses of an attic. If the truss is high, you can suspend wooden dowels, broom handles or even stout garden canes from it, to get a second level for drying. Chromium-plated dress rails, free-standing coat racks and hat racks are other possibilities. Bunches and single flowers can be hung on coat hangers first, to make maximum use of space.

Some flowers, such as astilbe, leeks, lady's mantle and goldenrod, and grasses can also be dried right-way-up, after being hung 'feet first' for a few days, to counteract the natural wilting that occurs. (Leeks, for example, entirely dried right-way-up develop a 'parting' at the top of the flower head.)

Chinese lanterns are best dried right-way up from the start, so the lanterns don't finish pointing upwards. Hang the stem on a clothesline, using the uppermost lantern as a hook. Wire mesh on a wooden frame placed across two trestles can support single flower heads while the stems hang beneath. Bracken stems can be placed in a cardboard box or large jar, with the fronds free standing in their natural shapes.

Many of the straw flowers – xeranthemum and helipterum, for example – have flower heads heavier than the dried stems can support. These stems are usually cut short and the heads wired (see page 27) before being hung to dry. Because the stem shrinks around the wire the latter is fixed firmly in position. However, staining and rust sometimes result, particularly noticeable in pale-coloured flowers, and a sensible compromise is to wire up partially dried flowers, while the stems are drier but still flexible.

Preserving by pressing

This is as simple as preserving by air drying, and many a school art project is based on colourful leaves pressed dry in newspaper. In fact, whole branches can be preserved this way, as well as ferns, bracken and spiky leaves, such as those of iris and montbretia. Pressing works best with leaves that are naturally flattish.

Pressing is the one method that retains brilliant autumn leaf colour, as well as the green of fresh beech. The drawbacks are that the finished material is rather more two dimensional than three dimensional, and very brittle. This flatness can be disguised by using the material with more rounded flowers and foliage. Individually pressed leaves, such as those of horse chestnut or paeony, may need wire stems or wire supports up the back, (see page 27). Flowers, of course, can also be pressed but these are used to create dried flower pictures, which are outside the scope of this book.

Technique
Place several pieces of newspaper or blotting paper flat, then carefully arrange the material in a single layer, making sure that no leaves overlap or curl, as they cannot be adjusted once dried. Cover with more layers of newspaper, interleaved with more foliage, if wished, and then place under a carpet. (On a smaller scale, press individual leaves between the pages of an old telephone directory.) For a less flat effect, build the layers up in an out-of-the-way corner, preferably somewhere warm and dry, and leave the weight of the newspaper to do the job. Check the leaves after a week; some may take up to six weeks to dry completely. Store in the paper until needed.

Preserving in a microwave
This relatively new method has proved successful with miniature roses or those with clusters of small flowers, such as 'Dorothy Perkins', in tight bud, small-flowered gypsophila and grasses. Other flowers may respond well to this method, and it is worth experimenting. Though the material must be air dried afterwards.

microwaving speeds up the process and also helps retain colour.

Technique
Strip away the foliage, then place the flowers or grasses in a single layer on several sheets of kitchen towel in the microwave. Use a medium setting (400-500W); three minutes is about right for gypsophila, and two and a half minutes for roses. Check after three minutes and replace the kitchen towel if it is soaked. Wipe the microwave after each use, as a lot of moisture is released. Remove the material, then hang it upside down, as for air drying, for about three days.

Preserving in water
This is really a variation of preserving by drying in air. Suitable candidates include fully mature, almost papery, heads of hydrangea; Bells of Ireland; proteas and heathers. Achillea is sometimes dried in this way, as are hosta leaves.

Technique
Strip the leaves, then place the flower stem in 2.5-5cm (1-2in) of water and, ideally, in warmth, to dry as quickly as possible. Do not top up the water as it evaporates and is absorbed.

Drying in Desiccants
Drying flowers in a desiccant is the least predictable method of preservation, which is why such flowers are extremely expensive to buy. It is also a connoisseur's method which, when successful, produces exquisitely lifelike flowers, in both form and colour. Desiccated flowers are more fragile and more

vulnerable to atmospheric moisture than those preserved by other methods, and are best displayed in airtight glass domes.

During desiccation, the water content of the flower is completely absorbed by the surrounding desiccant material. This can be silica gel, borax, alum, sand, or yellow cornmeal. Combinations of desiccants, such as equal parts by volume of cornmeal and borax, are sometimes used, as is clothes washing powder. Desiccants vary in weight and size of grain, and some are better for certain flowers than others. The desiccant should be heavy enough to keep the petals in position, as arranged, but light enough not to crush them. All desiccants can be re-used, provided that they are sieved regularly to remove any particles of dried flowers; and are thoroughly dried.

Silica gel is the most expensive desiccant, but gives the most reliable results. It is available from chemists and drug stores in both a granular and powdered form; the granular form can be pulverized with a rolling pin or in a food processer to provide the alternative powder. Silica gel is the quickest acting desiccant; thin-petalled and delicate flowers, such as pansies, may only need one day. Dry such flowers in powdered silica gel. Other, more rigid and substantial flowers can be dried in the granular form, and can take up to three weeks.

Borax and alum are powdery, lightweight and relatively inexpensive, but tend to form lumps when damp. If a petal is slightly wet on the surface, borax and alum sometimes harden and crack, exposing the petals to air; for this reason it is sometimes mixed with a rough substance, such as cornmeal. Flowers take nearer a week than a day to dry.

Sand is an old-fashioned desiccant, which needs careful preparation before use. It must be fine grain, clean and free of silt or salt; commercially packaged river sand is best. Sand is relatively heavy, which makes it unsuitable for many flowers and takes a long time – up to three weeks – to thoroughly dry the flowers.

Suitable flowers include garden roses, zinnias, delphiniums, daffodils, dahlias, carnations, marigolds, camellias and pansies. All should be picked in perfect condition, just before fully mature and on a dry day. The time lapse between cutting and inserting in a desiccant should be as short as possible. Cut the stem to within 2.5cm (1in) of the head. You can insert a short length of wire into the remaining stem, or wire it after drying. If the stem is woody, insert the wire directly into the base of the flower. Remove any remaining leaves.

The desiccant must be dry to start with; some silica gel is sold with a humidity indicator, or turns a colour if damp. If necessary, spread the desiccant in a thin, even layer in a shallow roasting tin and warm it for half an hour in a low oven, 120C/250F/gas ½. Dry desiccant after each use in the same way.

Put a 2.5cm (1in) layer of desiccant in the bottom of a plastic storage box or biscuit tin. Gently turn each flower in the desiccant to coat it, then place the flowers in the desiccant, in a single layer and not touching one another. Most flowers dry best placed heads up; bend any wires as necessary. Lay delphiniums and other spiky flowers lengthways onto the desiccant. Dry one type of flower at a time, as some flowers take longer than others.

Slowly pour a thin stream of desiccant over each flower, so that the space between every petal is filled and the flowers are covered. With open roses, carnations and dahlias, use a cocktail stick to separate the petals as you pour. Gently shake or tap the container from time to time, to get rid of any air pockets.

Continue sifting until there is a 2.5cm (1in) layer of desiccant over the flowers. Replace the lid tightly, then store in a warm, dry place. The warmer the desiccant, within reason, the quicker the drying and the less colour loss. Desiccants, especially sand, are sometimes heated in a very low oven immediately before using; and sometimes a flower-filled box or pan is heated immediately after being prepared, to hasten the drying process. There is obviously potential for microwaving, although any experimenting should be done with care and in a plastic, glass or ceramic container; never experiment with material you are not prepared to lose.

Thin-petalled, small and single flowers take less time to dry than thick-petalled, large and double-flowered forms. When the approximate drying time is reached, slowly pour out the desiccant through your hands. Catch and

inspect the first flower. If it feels papery, remove it and the others; if not return them for a few days to continue drying. A trick is to place one test flower slightly shallower than the others, but still covered, in the tin or plastic box, with a little marker. That way, it can be inspected without disturbing the others.

Flowers left too long in silica gel become very brittle and dark; those dried in other desiccants can be stored there without harm, although it is likely that the desiccant is needed for regular re-use.

Any desiccant clinging to the petals can be shaken away or brushed off with a fine paint brush.

Preserving with glycerine and antifreeze

Glycerine, diluted with water, is the traditional method for preserving mature foliage, especially beech, elaeagnus and eucalyptus. Glycerined material, whether whole branches or single leaves, retains its natural shape and flexibility, but glycerine is very expensive. Antifreeze diluted with water works in much the same way, and is less expensive. They are not, however, always interchangeable. Laurel leaves, for example, work well with antifreeze and not at all with glycerine.

Material treated with glycerine or antifreeze lasts indefinitely, and because of the leathery texture of the leaves, they can be dusted or even wiped with a damp cloth without risk.

Unlike air-dried material, which often retains much of its original colour, material treated with glycerine and antifreeze changes colour completely. Some material becomes pale and straw coloured, other material turns a rich mahogany brown or almost black, and there are various hues in between. Material treated in the dark tends to be a darker, richer shade than the same material preserved in a bright, sunny spot. The yellow or blue dye in antifreeze has no effect on the resultant colour of the foliage.

Technique
Choose only perfect leaves, and if preserving branches, remove any blemished or crowded leaves. To help stems take up the liquid, strip the bark off and split or crush the bottom 5cm (2in). Try to insert the stems into the preservative as soon as possible after cutting; if there is a delay, it is better to make a fresh cut. Foliage that is wilted before you start is high risk. To test whether a stem will take up glycerine or antifreeze, take a sample and stand it in water for a couple of hours; if the foliage wilts, discard it.

Dilute the glycerine or antifreeze with hot, or even boiling, water; the harder the stem, the hotter the water should be. Some people advocate two-thirds water to one-third glycerine or equal parts antifreeze and water, a proportion which is less expensive. As the glycerine is very thick, mix it thoroughly with water, or it will settle at the bottom of the container.

Choose a narrow, rather than a wide container, as only 7.5-10cm (3-4in) of preservative is needed. Narrow containers holding large branches may tip over, so support them if necessary. Top up the liquid as it is absorbed, making sure that it never dries out while the material is being preserved. Thick leaves can also be wiped with glycerine occasionally during the preserving process.

Large leaves, such as fatsia, mahonia, ivy and aspidistra, which are preserved individually, can also be floated in the solution of equal parts glycerine and cold water. Make sure they are fully submerged.

Glycerining or antifreezing can take from one to six weeks; generally, the thinner and smaller the leaf, the quicker it is preserved. Sometimes material – eucalyptus, for example – is very attractive before it is fully preserved, when only the veining is picked out in a contrasting colour. Semi-preserved foliage will not last indefinitely, though.

When the foliage feels smooth and has fully changed colour, and before drops of preservative appear on the leaf tips or surfaces, the material is finished. Because the preservative is absorbed up the stem, leaves at the top are the last to be preserved; it is best not to attempt hugely large branches, as the uppermost leaves may wilt before the preservative reaches them. Wiping these leaves with glycerine from time to time helps prevent curling and wilting.

Foliage that droops or oozes glycerine or is 'overdone', is liable to go mouldy in storage, or continue oozing liquid if there is any moisture in the atmosphere. Clean the leaves, by washing them in warm soapy water and dry thoroughly.

Cotoneaster berries and rose hips can also be preserved by placing the stems in diluted glycerine.

Buying Dried Flowers

Dried flowers are available from many florists, craft shops, market stalls, department stores and garden centres. Some of the new, fashionable home furnishing shops even sell bunches of dried flowers to tone in with their fabric ranges for each season. Wherever purchased, the rules for buying dried flowers are the same.

Buy dried flowers from a shop or stall with a rapid turnover, to get the best material. The dried flowers should be displayed out of direct sunlight, and with adequate space between each bunch; tightly compressed bunches are likely to have broken heads. Look first for strong natural colour, if appropriate, as this also indicates freshly dried material. Check for headless or broken stems; dried roses, for example, are often sold in bunches of twenty, and it is simply a matter of counting heads.

Check for flower heads kept in position only by the pressure of the surrounding cellophane or paper wrapping. Gently – in order not to damage the flowers or upset the florist – pull back the wrapping and give a very gentle exploratory shake. Flowers and seed heads harvested when over mature will be brittle and disintegrate into many pieces. Again, a gentle tap or shake should reveal any problems. Buy helichrysums with open but tight centres to the heads; the more of the central yellow showing, the older the flower was when it was dried, and, some people think, the less attractive. Check bulrushes and other large seed heads for splits and cracked pods.

If the stems are visible, check that there are no little black spots or other signs of mould. Holding the bunch firmly, turn it upside down; if masses of flowers fall out, the bunch is probably not worth buying.

The tiny flowers of gypsophila and broom bloom often fall off, but because the stems are tightly massed in a bunch, it can be hard to tell how many sprigs are flowerless. Compare two or three bunches, and pick the fullest.

Although many pre-mixed bunches are top-quality material, some are made up of ends-of-lines, with varying lengths of stems, and this is worth double checking.

If the weather is inclement, make sure a newly bought bunch is adequately wrapped; taking it home by public transport in the rush hour is asking for trouble.

If buying fresh flowers for drying at home, tell the florist what they are for, to get the freshest possible material in perfect condition. Ask specifically not to be given flowers that have been in cold store for some time, as they have a high water content, and are difficult to dry. Avoid, too, flowers with visible pollen, as this is a sign that the flower is nearing the end of its life.

20

There are no set proportions for mixed media arrangements. A small cluster of wired-up pine cones can enliven a bouquet of dried flowers; equally, a small cluster of dried flowers can become the focal point in a wide, shallow bowl filled with pine cones or attractive pebbles.

Whether a huge display of winter branches of lichen-covered larch or stag's horn sumach, with its crimson, velvety fruit cases, qualifies as a dried flower arrangement is a moot point. Categories and qualifications are irrelevant in all but competition or show work; what looks attractive is fine. The following are some of the more common non-floral additions; a great many more are available to the observant eye.

Cones
Pine cones are the most popular, but their use is often confined to Christmas time, when they receive a coat of silver or gold paint, or a bit of obligatory glitter. Pine cones are attractive, however, in their natural state and can be used all through the year. There are many varieties of pine cone, including the hugely long cones of the Mexican white pine. A trip to an arboretum or botanical garden is worthwhile for research; if consent can be obtained from a gardener for gleaning fallen cones, so much the better. Always ask first.

Larch is particularly useful because it is one of the few deciduous conifers. In winter, its dainty cones are displayed perfectly on the bare branches. Of the evergreen conifers, cryptomeria has even daintier cones, and in some forms the winter foliage turns a delicious reddy bronze or

purple – ideal as a filler for a dried flower display.

Fir cones vary enormously in size and shape; pick them when they come away from the tree easily and are fully ripe. Particularly lovely are the purple-brown cones of the bristlecone fir and the enormous cones of the noble fir. Spruce cones hang like lanterns from the branches and, similarly, vary in size and colour.

Gourds
These are a cheap source of colour and mass, especially for harvest-type displays. Although some people find gourds clichéd, redolent of '40s style two-tier formal arrangements, they have potential for imaginative use. Various sizes and shapes are available in green, yellow, orange, white and red, and there are packets of mixed seed for growing your own; look for them in the flower, not the vegetable, section of a catalogue or seed display, as ornamental gourds are inedible. Particularly attractive is the striped, turban-shaped type; most controversial is the warty type. A fully dried gourd feels very light in relation to its size, and gourds varnished before fully dried don't last. Varnishing with clear polyurethane gives an extra shine and does act as a preservative.

Ribbons
Though often considered among the most glamorous of florist's materials, using the wrong type of ribbon can spoil an otherwise attractive display. Florist's ribbon is usually acetate, paper, or plastic based, and is inexpensive. Firm and stiff, it can be

made into bows and trails with a crisp appearance and large, upstanding loops, but many people find its shininess incompatible with flowers, fresh or dried.

Silk ribbon is lovely, but less stiff, very expensive and not widely available. Satin is the name of a type of weave; satin ribbon is usually made of nylon, polyester or viscose thread. Of the three, polyester satin, which is starched, then heat treated to polish it, is the most widely available and firmest, and many people prefer it for general floral work. It is available in nearly 100 colours, in widths ranging from 1.5mm ($\frac{1}{16}$in) to 7.5cm (3in). Whatever type of ribbon is used, the best finish is to cut the ends at a sharp angle, not straight across or in a fish-tail shape.

Raffia
Raffia, available from craft stores and florists' sundries specialists, is inexpensive and useful for bulking up or as a decorative element of its own. Braided or tied crossways at regular intervals, it can form the basis for swags, wreaths or wall plaques, with flowers, foliage or cones interwoven into the braids. It is also useful for decorating woven containers, such as the ones shown on page 31.

Stones
Use pebbles and stones in miniature gardens; to camouflage stems in glass containers; and as ballast for large arrangements in lightweight containers. The same is true for washed gravel and granite chippings. Soft sandstones are unsuitable, as

they crumble and cause dust. Beach shingle and rounded flints found in river beds or available commercially as cobbles often have attractive colours and shapes. Granite chippings can be bought from builders' merchants and some garden centres. White marble chippings are available from builders' merchants but are not so generally stocked. Specialist tropical fish stockists often have a range of gravel for sale. Coloured gravel, like any dyed material, needs approaching with aesthetic caution.

Nuts

Use walnuts, hazel nuts, pecans, sweet chestnuts, Brazil nuts and almonds, in their natural state or sprayed with transparent gloss, in harvest baskets. For Christmas they are often sprayed silver or gold. To wire nuts for using on a swag, ring or wreath, put them in a vice, then drill a small hole and insert a single wire, pushed well in. Small nuts can be glued to the end of a wire.

Inedible but attractive nuts include horse chestnuts. Pick when their husks are half open and dry in their husks, a treatment equally suitable for sweet chestnuts, with their very prickly husks.

Moss

There are hundreds of species of moss, but only a few commonly available commercially. Sphagnum moss, which has largely been replaced by florists' foam as a foundation for wreaths, is sold fresh, and should be dried in a low oven, with the door left ajar, before being used with dried flowers.

Reindeer 'moss' or Icelandic 'moss' is a silvery grey lichen. Sold dry, florists often soak it in water before using, to make it more flexible. It can be used dry, but may need some of the soil-darkened lower bits cut off with a sharp knife.

The self-descriptive bun moss is rather difficult to come by ready dried, but is easily dried if collected fresh. It often grows on shaded roofs, but collecting it is definitely risky; it is easier to collect it from woods. Scrape off any soil adhering to the roots, then dry over a radiator or in an airing cupboard. It can be used fresh and will dry out naturally.

Lovely mosses can easily be found in most hedgerow banks beneath the grass, and even in the garden in the lawn. Remove soil, and dry in a warm room.

Paint, Bleach and Varnish

Some people consider painting dried flowers akin to heresy; others might occasionally paint a basket to match the flowers it contains, and others paint everything in sight. Car aerosol spray paints come in a range of colours, are easy to apply, relatively quick drying, and give a high gloss finish. Matt finish spray paints are also available. Both are particularly useful for delicate or highly intricate flowers. On the other hand, spray paints afford no control, and an all-over effect is inevitable. Sturdy material, such as seed heads of cow parsley, teasel, or cones, can be dipped in a solution of water-based emulsion.

Brushwork is slower, but the paint can be put on in graduated intensity, or in specific places, such as the centre of a flower or its petal tips. Poster paint gives a variety of finishes, depending on the type used (powder or acrylic-based).

Watercolours can produce an attractively subtle tint, best used on petal tips. Once dry, cover with varnish or polyurethane spray for permanence. Tubes of artist's oil paint thinned with linseed oil can also be used, but the paint may take several days to dry. For the adventurous, shoe polish is a possibility.

Teasels and pine cones can be bleached paler than their natural shade; submerge in neat bleach or a very strong solution for anything from a couple of hours to overnight, depending on the desired effect. Fully bleached material is a lovely ivory colour.

Varnishing hard materials, such as nuts and cones, enriches the colour and creates an attractively reflective surface. Try mixing natural and varnished material for an unusual effect. Clematis seed heads when sprayed with polyurethane retain their curled form, but become less fragile and more solid.

The following are the general supplies helpful in arranging dried flowers; supplies for drying and preserving, and wiring up, are covered elsewhere (see pages 12 and 26).

Wire mesh
15mm-2.5cm (½-1in) mesh galvanized wire is useful for large arrangements. Flowers and foliage inserted into wire mesh tend to find their own level and settle in position within the loose metal framework, often resulting in an informal, natural appearance. Absolute control over the material is diminished accordingly. Wire can also be used to protect florist's foam from breaking up in displays.

Wire cutters
These are available from hardware stores, and are generally useful, but florist's scissors (see below) do the same job.

Florists' foam
Florists' foam for dried flowers is usually grey or brown; that used for fresh flowers is usually green and is water absorbent. Florists' foam for fresh flowers can be used for dried work, but it is a softer consistency, and is more likely to crumble if you want to rearrange the dried materials. Both are available in blocks and preformed shapes, although the latter are more expensive. Blocks can be cut to shape, and although the shapes are unlikely to look as perfect as preformed ones, remember that ultimately they are completely hidden.

With florist's foam, stems remain exactly where they are inserted, with the result that arrangements can sometimes look explosive and angular. Lovely, curving arrangements can also be produced using this foam, and its reputation in this matter is perhaps a case of a poor workman blaming his (or her) tools.

Polystyrene is a cheaper alternative; its main drawbacks are that it breaks up rather easily, and is harder to push the natural stems into.

Knife
A knife is needed to cut and shape florist's foam, but any sharp kitchen or pocket knife will do.

Florist's scissors
There are several types of florist's scissors, of various sizes and shapes, with rounded and pointed tips, but all cut wires and virtually any dried material. They are all of a similar price, and the choice is entirely personal.

Secateurs
These are useful for general work, including cutting flowers for drying if you have no florist's scissors.

Frogs
Lead or plastic pinholders normally used for fresh work are unsuitable for dried flowers, as the material splits. You will need, however, plastic frogs, or florist's spikes, which impale the florist's foam to the base of the container and prevent movement. The frogs are available in several shapes and colours, and are

the flowers. The coating hardens and secures the arrangement permanently and adds weight.

Glue
Clear, quick-drying adhesive is generally useful for attaching errant flower heads to stems, fixing ribbons down, and so on. A refinement, but very expensive, is a hot glue gun. This looks like a fat pen, and works rather like a piping tube, releasing a small stream of special glue heated to 160C (360F). The glue dries very quickly, and can be highly controlled. It is especially useful for attaching heavy floral decorations to lightweight containers.

Rubbish bags
Baskets, in particular, should be lined with dark plastic, such as cut up rubbish bags, as bits of dried material tend to get caught in the open weave. If you are making large arrangements, the amount of rubbish created will also be large, and plastic bags are useful for instant disposal.

Dust sheets
If you are working on several arrangements, or a very large one, spread a dust sheet out first, around the area in question, to collect all the trimmings and odd bits and pieces.

String
Ordinary brown or white string is useful for binding moss to containers and re-tying bunches of flowers.

Cellophane tape
Both double-sided and single-sided tapes are useful for taping liners to the inside of baskets.

held in position by mastic.
An economical alternative, suitable for medium-sized or small arrangements, is to use a 2.5cm (1in) base of mastic, then insert two 90-gauge wires bent into hairpin shapes, curved-side down. Impale the florist's foam on the wires.

Mastic
There are several mastic products on the market. One is sold on a reel, and is the type normally used by professional florists; it is available from many florist's shops.
General purpose blue mastic is equally suitable. The surface of the container must be dry, to ensure firm adhesion. Mastic can be re-used, though it tends to harden with age.

Self-drying clay
A thin layer is spread over the surface of the florist's foam before inserting

Some people find the idea of wiring flowers, like dyeing or painting flowers, somehow morally wrong, or at least antiethical to the natural beauty that flowers represent. And some traditional wiring techniques used for fresh flowers – wiring rosebuds shut through their calyces so they can't open in the heat of a wedding, for example – do seem contrary to nature. On the other hand, discreetly replacing the broken stem of a flower with wire is sensible and economical.

Florists' wire, whether on a spool or in short straight lengths, is either blue annealed or tin-coated steel, rather like fuse wire. Confusingly, there are two systems of measuring the thickness of wire. The older standard wire gauge (SWG), sometimes called British wire gauge (BWG), is gradually being replaced by metric measurements. Often both measurements are given on the label, and many experienced florists still think in the old-fashioned SWG system.

Annealed reel wire, useful for binding flower stems into bunches and attaching moss or straw to a basket, comes in several thicknesses but the one most useful generally is 0.71mm (24SWG). Tin-coated or silver reel wire, sometimes called rose wire, is thinner and used for more delicate work, such as wiring individual florets or leaves. Reel wire can be cut to length for wiring flowers, and though economical, is time consuming; pre-cut wires are more convenient.

Long straight stem wires, called stub wires, are available in annealed steel, 17.5-35cm (7-14in) long, and

0.20-1.25mm (36-18SWG) thick; even more confusingly, the higher the gauge number, the finer the wire. For general work, 0.71mm (24SWG) or 0.90 (22SWG) is a good choice

Bent wires, or wire staples, are useful for attaching moss or lichen to florist's foam, for wreaths, rings, balls and so on.

Store the wires in containers heavy enough not to topple over, and keep in a dry place, to avoid rusting. If you

have several lengths and thicknesses, keep them separate, for ease of use.

Florists' stem tape is available in shades of green, brown and white. Some shades of green can be incompatible with the natural colours of dried material. Store tape in a cool, dry place, as heat tends to make it sticky.

Wire cutters or florist's scissors are necessary to cut reel wire and shorten stub wire.

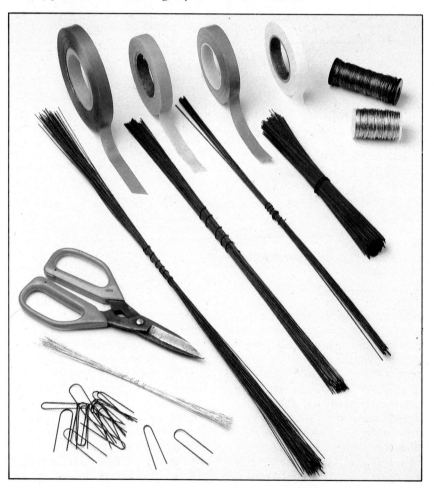

Wiring techniques

Although replacing weak stems is perhaps the most common reason for wiring dried flowers, there are other advantages. Several flowers or seed pods of one type, such as the blue statice and green chenopodium seed pods shown, can be wired together to get dense, tight bunches of colour. Bunching the natural stems doesn't have quite the same effect, as they radiate outwards and the longer the stem, the more difficult it is to maintain compaction.

Choose sprigs of flowers or seed pods with similar length stems – two, three or four sprigs is the usual number per bunch – then bend a wire roughly twice the length of the stems in half, making a right angle. Align one side of the wire along the tightly bunched stems, placing the bend just under the flowers or pods.

Bend the outward-pointing leg of wire back towards the stems, then twist it diagonally round and round the stems and straight wire, pinching it tightly at the bottom end.

Wiring can also extend a natural stem, which is done with the sprigs of blue statice shown, and also the pink-flowered phaenocoma. The bending and wrapping technique is the same as above, but use a suitably longer wire. In both cases, try to keep the wire as close as possible to the stem, and pinch it as tightly as possible (without damaging the stem) where the wire turns back.

Helichrysum is probably the most commonly wired flower, because the natural stems can be thick and unsightly, and tend to droop at the neck. Wiring isn't absolutely necessary and many of the helichrysums in the arrangements in

this book are used on their natural stems. In tightly packed displays, surrounding flowers can help support each other, to a certain extent; and in some cases, especially in a high-level display, the slightly nodding effect can be charming.

Helichrysums can be wired fresh, when it is easiest to insert the wire through the stemless head, but rusting, especially of pale-centred flowers, can result. Dry flowers can also be wired, but it may be difficult to penetrate the toughened heads with a wire stem. A good compromise is to dry the flowers for a week, then wire them and return them to finish drying. Whatever stage it is wired, push the wire up from the back, near the centre of the flower, then make a small hook at the upper end and pull the wire back down from the bottom, to secure the hook in the flower centre.

Either hide the wire in a hollow stem, such as that of grass, delphinium or dahlia, dried and saved for that purpose, or bind it with florist's tape. First wind the tape once or twice around the wire, just under the flower head. When it feels secure, begin winding it diagonally downwards around the wire, over-lapping slightly as you proceed. When the wire is covered, cut or tear the end of the tape, then punch the end.

Wire a pine cone by bending a wire into a U-shape around the lower section of the cone. Adjust the wire so it fits neatly within one concentric ring of scales, then twist the ends of the wire together. If the cones are to be used in a tight wreath, there is no need to tape the wires; if the wires will be visible, tape as above.

Every year in late winter or early spring, gardening articles in newspapers and magazines warn readers against getting carried away by seed catalogues, and buying seeds of far more plants than their gardens can ultimately accommodate. A similar warning, in modified form, applies to those who dry their own flowers and foliage; there is no point drying material, however easy it is, if there is insufficient storage space.

The enemies of all dried and preserved material are accidental physical damage; atmospheric moisture, which can lead to mildew and loss of texture; dust; significant temperature fluctuations, which cause condensation; overcrowding and overexposure to light. The ideal containers for air-dried and glycerined material are long cardboard florist's boxes, which have holes and allow air to circulate. Loosely pack bunches 'head to foot', first wrapping bunches in newspaper or tissue paper. A tiny sachet of desiccant placed at the bottom of the box helps keep the material dry during storage. However dry they may seem, thick stems or the centres of very densely petalled flowers may still contain some moisture.

Never store material in plastic, especially glycerined foliage, which inevitably contains a small amount of moisture which, trapped in the plastic, causes havoc. All dried material needs air, as the preservation process continues long after the initial drying or treatment process.

Label the boxes with their contents, to make retrieval easier, and store in a dry, frost-free and insect-free place; several boxes can be stacked on top of one another. Delicate or fragile dried materials are better stored as they are dried – hung upside down in loose bunches. Cones of tissue paper placed over the hanging bunches help keep off dust and light, while allowing for ventilation.

Dried arrangements are traditionally displayed from autumn to early spring, then replaced by fresh flowers until the following autumn. Although all dried materials can be successfully stored from one year to the next, the slow, natural process of senescence will affect the fibres and colours with the passage of time. Small and medium-size arrangements can be packed right way up in a cardboard box – a shoe box will hold several miniatures – with crumpled newspaper or tissue paper around the sides of the container to prevent movement. Cover with the lid or, if the arrangement is taller than the box, a loose dome of newspaper or tissue paper taped to the sides. Large arrangements may have to be dismantled, and stored as for newly dried flowers, above.

Desiccated flowers are the most fragile and vulnerable of all, and should be packed, heads up, and cushioned with tissue paper, in airtight tins.

A small, soft brush can be used to remove the dust from some of the more rigid air-dried materials. Glycerined leaves can be cleaned by wiping with a slightly damp cloth, which helps restore their sheen. Although dried flowers occasionally get damaged and broken, most never signal that they are well and truly finished, in the way that a bunch of wilted, smelly dahlias or daffodils, for example, do. Dried flowers fade with time, but many people find that the softened colours have their own charm, rather like old photographs. Also, initially strident colour combinations can become more harmonious simply by the passage of time and the fading that takes place. It is more likely that a dried flower arrangement is discarded because of boredom than because its useful display life is over.

Like throwing out perfectly good but much used clothes, this is a relatively minor self indulgence, compared to many human sins. There are, however, other options. The arrangement shown is made entirely of the broken-off heads of a two-year-old display, with the exception of a few newly dried love-in-a-mist seed pods, whose relatively fresh green colour is obvious. An exercise in economy but also creativity: a traditional, long-stemmed display is transformed into a contemporary 'heads and pods only' one, and given a new lease of life.

Transformations needn't be so drastic, and it is often a case of removing any damaged material, then rearranging the remaining flowers and foliage in a different container. Changing the location of the new arrangement-to-be often suggests a completely different approach. Incorporating new dried material with the old is another easy way of revitalizing useful but overfamiliar material, as is re-forming the original display into

two or three smaller ones.

Re-using sometimes involves repairing. The huge, central allium shown had developed a central parting and looked rather bedraggled. It was steamed for a few seconds over a kettle, then gently shaken, upside down, until the tiny thread-like stalks and seed pods re-settled into an evenly thick ball. Other flowers, such as dried roses,

can be re-shaped by hand in this manner, then allowed to dry fully before being used.

Broken-off petals can be re-attached to a flower head, using quick-drying clear glue applied from the end of a cocktail stick. Flowers dried in a desiccant often lose a petal or two in the drying process and, because this method of drying is the most difficult – and desiccant-dried

flowers the most expensive – it is usually worth attempting repair. Ordinary air-dried flowers, such as shasta daisies, that have lost a petal or two can still be used; remove the remaining petals, so only the velvety centre remains. Cone flowers often have their petals removed as a matter of course; their near-black, cone-shaped heads are an important component in the display shown.

Containers

The general requirements for a container for dried flowers are the same as those for fresh flowers; sympathetic in form, colour, scale and style to the flowers it will contain, and also to the room in which the arrangement is going to be displayed. It is rarely a question of an exact colour match, because flowers rarely have the flat single colour of a coat of paint or enamel. The colour in a flower – even a so-called 'self-colour', or one, all-over colour – can vary from the tip of the petal to the centre; as the light catches it; or with fading as the flower ages. Nor is it a question of exactly matching the style; a big bunch of dried echinops can look as attractive in a classical alabaster vase as a traditional formal arrangement.

Some flower arrangements, whether fresh or dried, are restful in feeling, while others are busy. Containers can match the feeling of the flowers, or contrast with it, but extremely hectic, multi-coloured arrangements in extremely ornate, multi-coloured containers can appear disconcerting. At the other extreme, a display of one type of dried flower in a completely unadorned container can take restfulness to the opposite extreme and result in a rather anonymous, bland feeling, the look of bunches of flowers waiting to be bought from a stall or shop.

Containers painted with images of flowers, such as the jug and wash basin shown, can provide the starting point for the selection of dried flowers for the arrangement. On the other hand, a literal translation of the floral images on a container into

dried flowers doesn't always work. Heavily stylized images of flowers can look peculiar compared to the real ones, whether these are dried or fresh. And very realistically painted or transfer printed, life-size images of a flower can make a dried flower look second best, in the same way that combining a dried and fresh flower of the same species often does.

As dried flowers do not need water, a variety of non-watertight containers can be used. Hairline cracked china is useless for fresh flowers, but fine for dried; quite lovely antique pieces can often be bought at affordable prices. Terra-cotta flower pots, complete with drainage holes, can hold informal dried flower displays as well as the more usual, formal lollipop trees. Woven baskets are the epitome of non-waterproof containers, and probably the ones most frequently used in commercial dried flower arrangements. Natural pieces of wood and bark offer more opportunities.

Because there is no need for water, which provides weight and stability, dried flower arrangements, especially large ones in lightweight containers, can topple over. Dried sand, pebbles, flower pot shards or marbles placed in the bottom of a lightweight container helps prevent mishaps later.

Dried flowers are on the whole rigid-stemmed, so there is no natural arching or drooping in an arrangement to break the line of the container, and informality can be difficult to achieve. Open weave containers, whether natural wicker

work or woven porcelain, are particularly suitable, because the dried flowers and foliage can be inserted between the weave as well as in the top. This was done with beech leaves and helichrysums in the arrangement on page 36, to soften the formality.

Another particular problem is the too-small neck syndrome. Some containers have a small neck in relation to their width, which can give an uncomfortable pinched look to an arrangement of erect-stemmed dried flowers. One solution is to insert a shaped block of florist's foam into the neck so that the foam is wedged tightly and protrudes from the top. Insert the stems into the florist's foam, angling them outwards and downwards as well as upwards, to hide the florist's foam and the thinnest point of the neck. Straight-sided, narrow-necked containers, have a natural elegance, but again, a piece of florist's foam protruding from the rim increases options enormously.

Another solution, if the neck is very narrow – a wine bottle or an old-fashioned ink bottle, for example – is to attach mastic and a florist's frog to the rim, then impale a large piece of florist's foam onto the frog. Alternately, make a ball shape of small mesh galvanized wire, which is filled with moss or foam, and wire this firmly to the top of the container.

Clear glass containers are considered incompatible with dried material, because they expose the basically ugly and bare stems. Glass containers lined with sphagnum moss, such as the battery jar on page 68, can work very well. Potpourri,

reindeer moss, dried fungi, sand, washed gravel and marbles can also be used as liners. If the glass is cheap or disposable, line it on the outside by glueing a dense layer of sphagnum moss or braided hay or other fabric evenly round the sides. Victorian opaline glass and milk glass are opaque and provide their own concealment, as do the darker, richer shades of Bristol and ruby glass.

Dried flowers can be displayed on a base, as well as in a conventional container. Traditional bases include velvet-covered card and sawn-through cross sections of pine or other wood, which will show the grain. A piece of felt should be glued to the underside, and florist's foam fixed to the top. Less conventional are an attractive section of cut wood, as shown on page 91; a round marble cheese board or rectangular marble pastry board, again with a central block of florist's foam fixed with mastic. A small chopping board of blocks of end-grain wood would make an attractive base; wood and dried flowers, like wicker work or bamboo and dried flowers, have a comfortable compatibility.

Scallop shells make pretty bases; the nautical overtones could be continued by filling the shells with a bouquet of dried sea holly.

Plastic containers, as well as being lightweight, have a visual and physical thinness which can look cheap. Particularly risky, in all senses of the word, are those moulded to look like classical vases, and can represent a very poor substitute. Familiarity can breed contempt, and anything reproduced by the thousands suffers accordingly.

Arranging Dried Flowers

Just as some people are instinctively good cooks or good with animals, some people know instinctively how to transform a bunch of flowers into an attractive display. Given a bouquet, perhaps without even thinking or being able to put into words what they are doing, their imaginations, hands and eyes work together to produce successful results.

Others have been trained, either professionally or in one of the many flower-arranging classes or societies that reflect the popularity of this art. Equipped with the rules and regulations of formal flower arranging, they can produce lovely arrangements that meet well defined criteria.

For many people, though, arranging flowers can be a real struggle. Such people often know what they like when they see finished arrangements, but have no idea how to go about creating them, and a great deal of frustration can result. For these people, recipe-type books on flower arranging, with the exact 'ingredients' of each arrangement illustrated set out, together with the method of assembly and order of procedure, offer great comfort.

Floral recipes, however, aren't always possible to follow. The chances of having an identical vase to the one shown are slim; the chances of having the exact setting and studio lighting in which the display was photographed to look its best are even slimmer. Having the same proportion and number of flowers as those used is also unlikely, particularly as flowers – including dried ones – can vary from one locality to the next, from one season to the next, and even from one year to the next. Like culinary recipes, sometimes substitutions have to be made or quantities changed, which is when panic can so easily set in.

Then, too, is the question of taste, which is at the core of flower arranging. Some books on the subject treat taste like a mathematical sum, with objectively correct and incorrect answers. Taste is even given moral overtones; that is, a certain arrangement might be good; another one, bad. And while some displays may conform to or flout the rules of formal flower arrangement, the question of taste is quite different.

In the end, taste is simply what you like and feel comfortable

with, not what a book says you should like. Obviously, the arrangements in this book, or any book, mirror the taste of the author, and, to some extent, the taste of the time. It is worth looking at old books on flower arrangement to see how much taste is affected by fashion – that most ephemeral of criteria.

The section that follows is designed to meet the needs of a wide spectrum of skills, tastes and attitudes towards flower arranging. The arrangements were done by several people, each with a great love of flowers but an entirely different approach; and the arrangements reflect their various skills and tastes accordingly. The arrangements range from the traditional to the adventurous; and from the exquisitely delicate and jewel-like to broad, abstract sweeps of colour and form. The arrangements are unlikely to appeal equally to everyone, but that is intentional. The aim is to expose the experienced, perhaps set in their ways, to new possibilities; and to help the novice clarify his or her own taste and sense of style.

There are instructions accompanying each arrangement, but also alternative choices of material; alternative approaches to the same floral brief; and the likely pitfalls to avoid. Lastly, the thinking behind the development of many of the arrangements is set out; valuable basic formulae that can be applied or adapted to an infinite number of variations on the floral theme.

Bouquet Basket

The bouquet on the previous page is made up of undyed, cottage garden-type flowers, foliage and seed pods, combined with wild material collected from woodlands, pastures and hedgerows. The bouquet has a natural colour compatibility – no flowers are terribly strident or out of key with the rest. Colours range from the white statice to the dark rich brown of glycerined beech foliage, with most of the material neutral beige and creamy browns. Soft, pastel colours are provided by the wired-up helichrysums.

Not all bouquets have this inherent colour unity and not all of the flowers from any bouquet have to be used in the same arrangement. Material which declares itself to be *outré* should be used in a little container of its own; saved until compatible material is at hand; or saved for spraying for Christmas decorations (see pages 96 to 103).

To make the display shown, the open-weave basket is lined first with sphagnum moss, then packed with florist's foam. The bouquet is divided into groups of similar types of material, and the general grouping is retained in the arrangement; nothing is scattered or peppered about. The first group to be inserted is the tall, spiky material – ornamental grasses, grains, artemisia, montbretia foliage, lychnis and poppy seed heads – which fills the back half of the basket, as far forward as the central handle. The idea is to create a good fan shape, with a dense cluster of teasels on one side, for interest.

The branches of glycerined beech foliage are cut into smaller pieces, then inserted directly in front of the handle, again in a roughly even fan shape. One tiny sprig is inserted between the woven vertical canes of the basket, on the right, to balance the visual weight of the teasels. The dark, rich colour of the beech creates a stage setting for the pale pastel helichrysum, white statice, wired-up pine cones, flax and golden achillea. The stems of these are cut short and are inserted next, to densely fill the front half of the basket. Think of the arrangement as a sort of three- or four-tiered seating, in which no one – or in this case, no flower – obscures the flower behind it.

The open weave of the basket offers an opportunity too good to miss, and a few helichrysums are reserved for wiring along the top row of wicker work, and around the side as well. Lastly, the florist's bow is wired to the centre. The quality of florist's ribbon varies. Some, such as the one shown, complement the flowers; others have a distinctly cheap and shiny look, and are better used with non-natural materials, or discarded.

Wired helichrysums sometimes get rust discolouring in the centre of the flowers, especially if they are wired while still fresh. Try to avoid these when buying ready-dried flowers, or use them in a less prominent position in an arrangement.

Informal Arrangements

Informal arrangements are built up by eye, and by the arranger's feeling towards the dried flower material, container, ultimate positioning and perhaps even sense of occasion. Informal arrangements can be harder to get right than formal ones, because there are no recipes or strict rules to follow. The main key to informal arrangements is having the right attitude; allowing the arrangement to develop of its own accord, and not imposing a preconceived solution upon it.

On the whole, there is safety in generosity. An arrangement is more likely to be disappointing because it contains too little material than too much. This does not mean that a large arrangement is bound to be better than a small one, but that, whatever the size of the arrangement, the flowers should not be presented as lonely single stalks, with masses of air between one flower and the next. If in doubt, keep adding material; you can always remove any excess, if necessary. And although some large flower heads, such as alliums, garden roses, hydrangeas and paeonies look odd if partially obscured, smaller ones can look most attractive overlapping one another. An arrangement of dried flowers is a total composition, not a line up of specimens waiting to be identified.

It is also generally more sensible to use a limited range of flowers for any one display, rather than taking a 'one of each' approach, and using as many different flowers as possible.

It is harder to achieve a feeling of informality and gently curving shapes with dried flowers than with fresh, because the stems of most dried flowers are poker straight. One solution is to use flowers of different heights, so that shorter flowers obscure the stems of taller ones behind. Although it can seem wasteful shortening a long stem, it is often necessary for the finished effect. Using naturally curving or arching dried material, such as sprays of beech leaves, ivy or hellebore leaves, hops and lamb's tongue stems, is another alternative.

Finally, informal isn't the same as messy and, as any fashion designer knows, a great deal of time, effort and thought can go into a seemingly effortless and relaxed finished effect.

This is not an arrangement that can be copied easily, simply because so much depends upon the container, a parian bust of Queen Victoria made in 1897, to commemorate sixty years of her reign. Although the bust was mass produced as a souvenir, this one is unique, because the parian crown which formed part of the original design has been lost – unfortunate in terms of the value, but an incentive to create a floral crown instead.

One perfect hydrangea flower head – a mixture of soft greens, blues, pinks and mauves – is topped by spikes of lavender, dill and white delphinium. The sub-structure is the usual block of florist's foam impaled on a frog fixed to the top of the head with mastic.

The possibilities for alternative combinations are many: old-fashioned garden roses dried in silica gel and arranged with various dried ferns; an exotic mixture of proteas, banksias and eucalyptus foliage; a simple massed bunch of velvety red celosia. Queen Victoria could be crowned for Christmas with conifer foliage bejewelled with bright red dried dahlias or rose buds; and for Easter with pale lemon mimosa, golden rod and lady's mantle with some yellow and white ribbons, for added attraction. Whatever the choice of raw material, it is best used informally, even humorously. The bust exudes formality and, if topped by an equally formal flower arrangement, might well appear overbearing.

This little woven basket could just as easily be placed in the chapter on hanging decorations. The siting of an arrangement and its level of formality are equally important considerations, and any categorization is bound to favour one at the expense of the other. Nevertheless, this basket is an exercise in informality, with its profusion of achillea, helichrysum, statice and dyer's greenwood. None of the material is wired, the natural stems simply being inserted into florist's foam.

What lifts this arrangement out of the ordinary, and adds a delicacy, is the use of wild rose hips and red-dyed lesser quaking grass. The former is often preserved with glycerine, but untreated hips, such as those shown, remain attractive for some weeks, especially in a cool room. Any that do shrivel can be removed and replaced by fresh hips or dried seed heads. Spraying rose hips with varnish or hair lacquer is also said to increase their useful life. The dyed quaking grass is perfectly at home surrounded by similarly coloured natural flowers; dyed colour isn't automatically bad colour.

The rich reds, oranges and golds of this arrangement are autumnal in feel and, because the basket is small, changing the flowers for each season would be a relatively inexpensive exercise. A winter selection could include a few larch branches, wired pine cones and seed pods, such as those of poppy, grape hyacinth or the brilliant seed pods of *Iris foetidissima*. One or two velvety maroon seed heads of sumach would add a change of scale. Spring could be heralded by a generous display of dried mimosa; fresh mimosa dries naturally in water, so it is a more economical purchase than would at first appear. In summer, the basket could be filled with dried mint, lavender, hollyhocks and garden roses, perhaps punctuated by the intense blue of dried cornflowers.

Circular tables call for all-round displays, and a basket of flowers is a tried and true solution. An informal arrangement, such as the one shown, is also a token of hospitality, and is particularly welcoming in an entrance hall or living room.

Arching spikes of silvery white artemisia feature heavily in this arrangement. Artemisia is an unruly plant in the garden where its slender stems are often toppled by the slightest summer wind. Artemisia is equally unruly in dried flower arrangements (it quickly wilts when used fresh), but, like a wayward child, is charming all the more for it. Its unregimented curves and twists

relieve the poker straightness of other dried flowers, in this case, pink and mauve statice.

Statice is cheap, cheerful and colourful, but has its own built-in drawback; that of overexposure. When statice is used as the backbone of a floral display, it often helps to introduce at least one unusual component to add interest. In this arrangement, artemisia, the fluffy seed heads of hare's tail grass, small thistles and a sprig of dried cotton lavender do that job.

Some people find the rather astringent aroma of artemisia too strong, and sprigs of lavender could be used to overcome that problem,

as well as to provide delicate touches of colour.

There are various stages at which any flower arrangement can be said to be finished, although eventually there is a danger of over-working it, so that it loses its freshness. In this arrangement, ribbons of toning pink or mauve could be worked round the handle of the basket, or small bows tucked into the arrangement. A small wreath, encircling the base of the basket, could be made of statice, artemisia and phalaris, to continue the floral theme downwards and also visually widen the rather narrow base of the basket in relation to the spread of the dried flowers.

Some containers are colourless, in the larger sense of the word, taking their character from the flowers they hold. Other containers, such as the Victorian glazed ceramic cache pot shown, have vibrant personalities of their own, and flowers should be chosen and arranged in response to that strength. Having an unusual container is not a limitation but a challenge, which can be met in many different ways.

The three neo-classical female figures taking the weight of the central container are direct references to the classical caryatids, such as those found on the Acropolis. Caryatids acted as columns, supporting the great weight of the roof above, and, even on this tiny scale, a visually weighty flower arrangement seemed a good solution.

Interestingly, the first arrangement made for this container was the one shown on page 67, composed of the balloon-like love-in-a-mist, lady's mantle and chenopodium. The combination looked far too light and airy, as if the good ladies were bearing no weight at all. Moved lock, stock and barrel, including the wire mesh foundations, into the simple blue bowl, the arrangement seemed much more at home. Always be prepared to admit a false start or mistake and try other options.

Although the overall effect of the flowers and grasses is that of a medley, these are used in clusters, or mini-bunches, to keep the medley from becoming a confusion. The one exception is the ornamental onion, which is large enough to make a statement on its own. The mini-bunches are built up on a small mesh wire framework, with sprays of grasses and lavender wired together as mini-bunches, and evenly distributed to break the general outline and density of the display. The resulting arrangement has a richness and ornateness typical of late Victorian design, and the flowers and cache pot complement one another.

A completely different approach would be to contrast the intricacy of the container with a simple display of flowers; blue or pink delphinium spikes; a huge mass of gypsophila and helipterums; or dried hollyhocks or African marigolds, both Victorian favourites. As with the bust of Queen Victoria (see page 39) an informal arrangement best complements this potentially overbearing container.

Many dried flower arrangements have overtones of country gardens, because much of the material used is grown in traditional English-style gardens, whether the gardens are in temperate regions of Australia, New Zealand, South Africa, America, Europe or England itself. The flowers don't necessarily originate in England – garden delphiniums, for example, are hybrids of species ranging from Siberia to the Pyrenees, and paeonies, those most English of flowers, have their origins in Siberia, China, Tibet and Mongolia.

More unusual, but no less attractive, is the wealth of dried flowers and seed heads from the Southern Hemisphere, largely Australia and South Africa. Importing and exporting dried flowers is a world-wide trade, and material from the Southern Hemisphere is becoming ever more popular in the North. Like 'English' dried flowers, they are available far from their country of origin.

The handsome arrangement shown is composed entirely of imported Southern Hemisphere material. Included are the flowers and foliage of Australian honeysuckle; hakea foliage; Cape honey flower; willow myrtle; craspedia; red bottlebrush and dryandra.

The display is based loosely on an asymmetrical triangle, and is built up densely on a foundation of florist's foam. Because the material is so bold, and ranges in quality from the delicate to the huge, it is roughly grouped, rather than tightly bunched, as in the white Victorian cache pot (see opposite). Groups of

flowers overlap, interweave and drift through one another. The broad band of red craspedia, added towards the end, emphasises the diagonal.

It is an exuberant display, not a restful one, but the exuberance is well controlled. For a country-style rendition, use huge heads of globe artichoke; the smaller but similar pink cardoon; ball-shaped echinops heads; spikes of rat's tail statice or cat's tail grass; sea lavender; heather; butcher's broom and statice.

A wicker basket or pottery container would also give a softer feeling to this display, and would help to set off the brilliant colours of the tropical flowers.

The 'I don't know much about art but I know what I like' approach to aesthetics is as valid in the field of flower arranging as in any other. It is also true that the more unusual a flower arrangement is, the more likely to evoke a strong response, whether positive or negative. The outrageously unique parrot arrangement shown is a good example; it is either a *cause célèbre* or a *bête noir*, depending on personal taste.

The painted plaster container is an Edwardian calling card holder, its rock-like, shallow base flattened to receive visitors' cards. Here it holds a simple arrangement of olive-green dyed hare's tail grass and dyer's saffron, inserted into florist's foam impaled on a frog fixed to the base with mastic.

Neither the grass nor the curiously shaped dyer's saffron flowers could be said to be pretty, in the traditional sense of the word, but neither is the container; both reflect the exotic character of the other. The simple, sweeping shape of the grass repeats the graceful curve of the parrot's back and tail, and the orange stamens of the dyer's saffron repeat the touches of orange in the parrot's eye.

A less controversial solution might be to make a large, informal arrangement of dried grasses and leaves in natural colours; barley, large and lesser quaking grass, meadow foxtail, timothy and Yorkshire fog, for example, with a few sword-like leaves of montbretia for accent. The parrot would then become a semi-hidden presence, rather than a dominant one.

Not every flower arrangement has to make a dramatic statement, and the informal cottage-garden approach makes a pleasant respite. Taste in dried flower arrangement, like taste in food or fashion, should be broad enough to encompass many styles, even quite modest ones.

This old-fashioned, unpretentious china jug and wash basin presents a ready-made colour scheme. The pinks, greens and whites of the floral motif are repeated in the colours of the sea lavender, helichrysum, love-in-a-mist and phalaris seed heads, delphinium and the sharply pointed foliage of the butcher's broom. The latter, an unexpected member of the lily family, produces tiny green flowers in the centre of its leaves, which are technically cladodes, or leaf-like branches. Preserved in glycerine, butcher's broom becomes a deep, creamy beige; air-dried, it retains its green colour. It is also sold dyed in various colours, some more believable than others.

The roughly triangular arrangement is built up on a florists' foam block, tightly wedged into the jug. There is no particular focal point, but no restlessness, either, just a pretty compilation of colours and shapes. The tallest stems are inserted upright in the centre of the arrangement, and lower and shorter stems gradually splay outwards towards the base. The stems of the lowest flowers are angled slightly downwards, to conceal the rim of the jug, and soften the outline shape.

A more literal interpretation of the floral motif could be carried out with garden roses, although these are a rare commodity.

Formal Arrangements

Formal arrangements, whether of dried or fresh flowers, go in and out of fashion quite regularly. At the moment, the 'in' approach is an informal one, broaching, in extreme cases, on the dishevelled. Perhaps this is a reflection of the informality of contemporary manners and other aspects of social behaviour. Nonetheless, fashion is a very fickle judge; formality in flower arrangements and other aspects of daily life has a great deal to offer and no doubt, in due course, will be 'rediscovered'. Important occasions can be made more emphatically so with formal flower arrangements, and the well defined geometric shapes – round, L-shaped, triangular, Hogarth curve – offer a starting point and sense of direction for those in need of it. Then, too, the art of flower arranging involves a wide spectrum of responses, not simply formal or informal. An arrangement that starts out formal may become more relaxed part-way through, and end up semi-formal, loosely based on a geometric shape. Or a 'non-arranged', tumbling bunch of flowers may start to develop a loosely rounded outline in the course of arrangement. Use the rules of formal flower arranging as reference points, but respond first and foremost to the flowers themselves.

Formal L-shaped Arrangement

Dried flowers lend themselves to formal arrangements because they have no will, or indeed life, of their own. Unlike fresh tulips, for example, whose stems twist into fantastic shapes and whose flowers open out as they age, a flower preserved in silica gel remains unchangingly as it was when first arranged. The straight stems that are a result of air drying also fit in well with the geometric rigidity that many formal arrangements require.

People often spend a great deal of time and effort trying to inject a feeling of informality, even a slight unruliness, into their dried flower arrangements, and regard straight stems as a handicap, not an asset. Formal arrangements, though, have their rightful place in interior decoration, and certain occasions, whether a dinner party at home or a grand ball, are given a heightened sense of formality by their presence.

Formal arrangements of dried flowers needn't be intimidating or boring. Fresh and unusual combinations of material, such as that in the L-shaped arrangement shown, help overcome the predictability that formal arrangements sometimes have. Tiny personal touches, such as the miniature formal arrangement nestling under the 'parent' one, help overcome the anonymity also associated with formality.

The material in the display, all on natural stems, is built up on a foundation of florist's foam. The height and width – twice that of the container – and general triangular shape, is established first, with the spikes of grey-green oat grass. The delphinium, bleached barley, achillea, and Chinese lanterns are added in sequence, radiating upwards, outwards and downwards from a central point. The closer to the centre the material, the shorter the stems. There is no focal point, just an even distribution of contrasting colours and shapes within the triangular outline. A few relatively wayward sprigs of hazel and silver-grey artemisia, added almost as an afterthought, add interest within the formal framework. The miniature arrangement is made in the same way as the large one, except that little strips of Chinese lantern are wired up to take the colour theme through.

The potentially harsh combination of yellow, orange and blue is softened by the grey-green grasses, silver artemisia and bleached barley. Using that same neutral material as a background, cream zinnias, pink delphinium and pale-pink achillea could be substituted for the more intensely coloured material; or white delphinium and bleached phalaris, bleached poppy heads and bleached broom bloom.

The Hogarth curve, or lazy S, is a popular formal shape but difficult to do in dried flowers unless done on a very large scale, because tight curves are awkward to create, given rigid stems. A symmetrical or asymmetrical triangle or all-round circular arrangement is simpler, and would also suit the flowers used in this display.

Mix and Match

Dried flowers, foliage and seed pods are potentially excellent mixers. They are akin to fresh flowers and foliage, having once been alive themselves; but like artificial material, both can theoretically last indefinitely. When mixing and matching, there is nothing to beat trial and error, and some of the displays shown were re-arranged several times, using different proportions and combinations of material, to achieve a satisfactory result.

Opportunity also brings constraints, and there are some things that dried material cannot do. If dried stems are submerged in water, they will rot and their useful life is shortened. There are ways of overcoming this problem, such as placing a water-filled receptacle for the fresh flowers inside a larger, dry one, as in the combination of fresh flowers and preserved foliage shown.

Although it may be philosophically interesting, combining fresh and dried specimens of the same plants – fresh and dried roses, for example – rarely works; the dried material usually comes out looking second best, a pale ghost of its former living self. A bowl of fresh roses surrounded by a shallow ring of dried rose-petal potpourri might be very effective, though, as the petals no longer 'read' as roses, but as a delicately scented texture.

As well as fresh and artificial flowers, any inherently attractive organic forms, such as moss, pebbles, nuts or shells and even feathers, make natural partners for dried flowers and foliage. Most adults, when confronted with an unusual menu or combination of ingredients, are prepared to try anything once, and are often pleasantly surprised. The same attitude, applied to mixing and matching flowers, can produce equally refreshing results.

Whatever the size of a garden, there is usually more foliage available than flowers. When there are no fresh flowers at all, as in the depths of winter, garden foliage and dried flowers make a splendid combination. This little arrangement was done in winter, albeit a mild one, and instead of evergreens, the thickly felted white leaves of cineraria were used.

Cineraria, or silver leaf, is a sun-loving semi-hardy shrubby perennial, but is often grown as a half-hardy annual. It is worth leaving a few plants in the ground over winter, as a source of cut foliage. There are various cultivars, including 'Silver Dust', with silvery, ferny leaves; 'White Diamond' and 'Ramparts', both with deeply cut foliage.

To prevent wilting, the tips of the stems were inserted, immediately after cutting, into boiling water for a few seconds; they can also be singed over a flame. The prepared stems were then placed in a deep container of water for several hours, to complete the conditioning.

The old ginger jar used for this arrangement is half filled with water. This meets the needs of the cineraria, while the dried flowers – sprigs of pink heather and deep-pink xeranthemums, both on natural stems, and silvery-blue echinops, on wired stems – are inserted so their stems rest above the water line. An unconventional approach and fiddly task, but it allows the foliage to remain fresh while the dried material remains dry, and can be used again and again.

Other grey-leaved garden shrubs that could be substituted include the hardier *Senecio greyi,* more correctly *Senecio* 'Sunshine', with its tough, rounded leaves, white felted underneath; and lavender cotton, with its finely divided, thread-like foliage. The senecio needs its woody stem hammered before being immersed in water; lavender cotton should be prepared as for cineraria.

Fresh heather, such as the winter-flowering cultivars, could be used in a similar arrangement, and left to dry naturally with their stems in the water.

For a colour scheme based on blue and silver, dried cornflowers and lavender could replace the xeranthemums and heather. For one based on yellow and silver, use African daisies and cluster-flowered everlastings.

Artificial flowers and dried flowers have a special affinity; the former have never lived and the latter are dead but, used together, they can create a display as handsome as any composed of fresh material. In practical terms, there is no problem of some stems needing water and others needing to be kept dry.

Artificial flowers sometimes have unnatural colours and, when used on their own in a massed display, a disturbing frenzy of colour can result. The vast majority of dried flowers have more subtle, muted natural colouring and, as in this arrangement, help tone down the colour scheme. Both the dried and artificial material have to be roughly the same key, because too-bright artificial flowers combined with too-muted dried flowers can give disappointing results, with the artificial flowers appearing even more stridently artificial, and the dried flowers appearing dowdy.

In the blue and white arrangement shown, creamy white statice, silver grey artemisia and translucent white honesty tone down the not-quite-believable blue of the silk African lilies and the blue-flowered broom. The subtle variations in the whites of the dried material also help dilute the flat, dazzling, 'soap-powder commercial' white of the fake poppies. The leaves of the artificial flowers are tucked out of sight, as they add nothing to the display.

Florist's foam impaled on a frog fixed to the base of the container with mastic forms the foundation. White gypsophila, xeranthemums and clematis seed heads would be equally attractive.

Combining cut flowers and house plants in a single display is called *pot et fleur,* and little baskets or plastic bowls filled with plants and cut flowers are standard florist's wares. The flowers are usually fresh, though, and bunched together so that their stems can be inserted in one water-filled container or piece of florist's foam concealed in the compost. Fresh flowers are sometimes used singly, inserted into water-filled florist's vials, test tubes or even empty cigar cases, but these need frequent refilling. Sooner or later, the flowers themselves need replacing.

A *pot et fleur* based on dried flowers has no such drawbacks. Because the flowers are technically already dead, they don't need replacing. And because the flowers are not dependent on water, they can be placed wherever they look best, even wired along the stems, as is done in the *pot et fleur* shown.

The flowers – helichrysum, achillea, statice, morrison and lady's mantle, in a rich range of yellows and oranges – are concentrated at the top of the plant, where the stems are simply inserted in the compost. Although a certain amount of moisture is taken up from the compost, it is not enough to harm the dried flowers, provided any wire stems are wrapped with waterproof tape, to prevent rusting. Watering the plant used in a *pot et fleur* from the bottom minimizes the problem.

The density of the flowers is decreased gradually, with a few attached loosely to the woody stems of the grape ivy with silver wire. Grape ivy is a tough, tolerant plant,

and there is little risk of damaging the stems, if you proceed with care. The tips of the stems are soft, new growth, and should not be decorated.

Other suitable trailing plants include the plume asparagus, and the ordinary asparagus fern. Sprigs of gypsophila wired to the stems would complement their delicate ferny foliage. An out-of-flower indoor jasmine could be dressed up with sprigs of velvety round stirlingia heads.

The brick pier on which the

trailing plant is displayed is an unlikely feature of ordinary homes, but a kitchen stool, old-fashioned wooden high chair or high shelf would do equally well.

Non-trailing plants can also be dressed up; the bare lower stems of aspidistra, for example, could be concealed in a thicket of bleached white amaranthus spikes. Even an out-of-flower African violet, normally a dull sight, would be greatly enhanced given the company of a few tiny star-like glixia flowers, until its own blossom appeared.

Fresh Flowers and Dried Foliage

Although dried or otherwise preserved foliage has a great deal to offer, it doesn't combine easily with fresh foliage. Fresh greenery usually makes preserved foliage look dead by comparison. Trying to use glycerined beech and yellow-variegated elaeagnus leaves with fresh roses and chrysanthemums in one arrangement proved the point, but the challenge was easily met and a very interesting arrangement is the result.

Stripping and discarding fresh leaves is not as bizarre as it first seems, because, in this case, both the rose and chrysanthemum leaves are quite dull looking. Removing the leaves has the additional benefit of reducing transpiration and thus extending the life of the flowers, and is standard practice when conditioning florist's chrysanthemums, dahlias and forced lilac and viburnum.

The logistical problem of keeping the stems of the fresh flowers in water, while keeping the stems of the preserved foliage dry, is solved by putting a glass tumbler of water in the centre of the brass container, to hold the rose and chrysanthemum stems. The foliage stems and grain stalks are inserted into wire mesh packed between the inner and outer containers. This foundation is reflected in the arrangement; an inner cluster of fresh flowers surrounded by an outer ring of dried foliage and grain. It is important to use a generous amount of material, so that the two components overlap and form an integrated whole. The densely packed white spider chrysanthemums hide their stems.

Some dried seed heads have a slightly fantastic appearance, as if they were designed by art students, rather than a product of nature. Arrangements based entirely on the seed pods of love-in-a-mist, teasel, poppy, lotus flower or annual scabious can look like small abstract sculptures.

Equally extraordinary are fantasy feather flowers, such as the pheasant-feather flowers that are the centre of interest in the pair of small arrangements illustrated. The flowers are made from the soft breast and back feathers of pheasant or partridge, wired in concentric circles to a central core of artificial stamens. A wire stem is attached, then taped. Feathers of the wood pigeon or domestic chicken add more variety. Long tail feathers of pheasant can also enhance an autumnal arrangement. Peacock tail feathers are occasionally used in very large dried flower arrangements, but their size and intensely metallic blue-green colouring tends to make the dried material look dowdy.

Glycerined beech leaves and broom bloom, inserted into florist's foam, form the bulk of the display, which takes its colour cue from the containers – hand-made pottery vases with oval bases especially designed for narrow shelving. Honesty and poppy seed heads and the faceted round seed heads of annual scabious, sometimes called the pincushion flower or paper moon flower, continue the colour theme. The scabious seed heads, which resemble tiny satellites, are rarely available commercially, but can be grown annually from seed.

The seed pods need careful handling, though, as little sections break off at the slightest touch, when they are ripe.

Fantasy flowers range from the almost believable to the bizarre, and should not be dismissed, simply because they are not real. Little larch cones can form the centre of fantasy flowers, with 'petals' of hornbeam, maple or ash keys glued in between the lower scales, or 'petals' of honesty seed heads glued around a centre of sea holly or rudbeckia. Small sprigs of feathery grass seed heads, such as reed or pampas grass, can be glued into the little holes all round the top of a poppy seed head, to form a fantasy flower similar to a spider chrysanthemum. Simpler still are tulip-like fantasy flowers made by cutting open the orange seed pods of Chinese lantern.

A pine cone or large rose hip makes a good centre, with husks from sweet corn forming the petals.

The chances of having spring-flowering dogwood and summer-flowering shasta daisies and African lilies in bloom at the same time in the same garden are virtually nil. Thanks to the wonders of modern manufacturing, however, silk facsimiles of each can be combined in a pleasing display without any reference to natural seasons. The arrangement shown is based on the white forms of these flowers and the rich, autumnal hues of preserved beech – both ordinary and the darker copper form – and laurel. Laurel, being evergreen, has no autumnal hues of its own but is transformed into a rich mahogany brown, by preserving with antifreeze.

An inner circle of tightly packed sprays of broom bloom adds bulk to the framework of foliage. The broom bloom also provides a delicate contrast to the silk flowers, which were added last. Though modest in itself, broom bloom is invaluable in setting the stage for more dramatic flowers and seed heads; it is a bit like gypsophila, but tougher and denser. As well as its natural beige hue, used here, broom bloom is available bleached white and dyed.

As with the blue and white arrangement, the fabric leaves in this display are concealed as much as possible, because green dyes tend to call attention to their own artificiality.

White silk iris, lilacs and apple blossom could be substituted for the flowers shown. For a higher key display, orange-red silk dahlias, chrysanthemums and tulips could be used, perhaps together with bronze-dyed eucalyptus leaves. Using silk flowers of several colours is always tempting, but it carries a risk. The subtle variations and shades of brown in the preserved foliage could not compete against a riot of fierce colours, and the end result might well be restless and lacking in unity.

Hearts and Flowers

Valentine's Day and gifts of flowers are inseparable, and roses are the most symbolic floral love token of all. In the vocabulary of the Victorian Language of Flowers, forty different species and cultivars of rose were each assigned a specific message of love. The Austrian rose, for example, meant 'Thou art all that is lovely'; the 'Boule de Neige' rose meant 'Only for thee'; and 'La France' meant 'Meet me by moonlight'. Different coloured rosebuds had their own special meanings, and a bouquet of mixed roses could convey complex messages and great sentiment.

Although the Language of Flowers is no longer used, the red and pink dried rosebuds that help fill the glazed porcelain *coeur a la crème* mould convey a clearly romantic message. The arrangement is an ideal Valentine's Day gift for someone who enjoys cooking as well as sentiment – both the flowers and their container remain attractive long after Valentine's Day.

Reindeer moss is packed in first, and the rose buds and helipterums rested in the crevices of its uneven surface. Few flowers are needed; the pink rose buds were extracted from a single scoop of rose-petal potpourri. Pink and rose-red ribbon bows complete this, and the alternative arrangement of dried moss in a woven wicker basket, with a cluster of bright red craspedia heads and pink, daisy-like phaenocoma. The heather-like foliage of phaenocoma is detached from the woody stem and used separately.

Hanging Decorations

Dried flowers displayed on walls are subject to the same criteria as dried flower arrangements anywhere else. They should be large enough, either singly or in a group, to make an impact, but not so large that they become unwieldy. Wall- or ceiling-hung dried flowers should be well away from the dangers of passing domestic traffic, although not so distant that they are difficult to see. Although weight is unlikely to be a problem, the display should be firmly fixed.

For large-scale, room-set type displays, with an equally large budget, you could fill the four corners of a ceiling with arrangements, with or without swags between. A huge central ceiling rose could be constructed with dried flowers, in much the same way that classical ceiling roses were picked out in plaster work. Arrangements, whether formally symmetrical or casual, placed over a door or window, or even over a large piece of furniture, act like floral architraves, emphasizing the feature beneath.

Rooms in older homes often have high ceilings and picture rails. Instead of pictures, hang dried flowers in clustered displays; use toning ribbons for support.

Lastly, generous, not-yet-arrranged bunches of dried flowers, either of one type or mixed, are attractive enough to be hung without embellishment, from brackets or rafters, especially in an informal setting, such as a country-style living room, hall or bedroom. If conditions are right (see page 12), fresh flowers hung up to dry can do double duty as an instant display.

Large Wreath

Although wreaths are automatically associated with Christmas festivities and more sombrely, funerals, there is no reason why they shouldn't form part of the everyday language of flower decorations. Dried-flower wreaths are, of necessity, indoor features, unless you are prepared to move them in and out, as the weather dictates. A well covered porch would be suitable, though.

The wreath shown is made of dead, lichen-encrusted larch branches, gradually built up over a wire mesh tubular circle base. Dead branches can be quite brittle, but these were collected after weeks of soft English rain, which made them pliable enough to use. In the final stages, creamy pink helichrysum and beige happy flowers are woven into the wreath, bird's-nest fashion, together with an occasional grass seed head. The flowers diminish in density towards the top of the wreath, so that the attractive structure of the larch branches is not completely hidden.

Larch, a deciduous conifer, is particularly suitable for such wreaths. When dormant, it provides charming clusters of small cones on bare branches, without the bother normally associated with shedding conifer needles. Vine stems, either grape or ornamental, and clematis stems, either of vigorous-growing garden types, or the wild clematis could be substituted for the larch. These stems can be wound round several times to build up a circular base, without the need for wire mesh. For the economy-minded, annual prunings of over-vigorous growth can be transformed, while

still supple, into wreath bases, for immediate use or stored for later use.

Other possible sources for natural ring bases include the colourful young growth of willows, such as the scarlet willow, with bright red shoots; and the yellow, or golden willow. The bright green slender stems of kerria are often considered a menace in the garden, where they sucker everywhere; use them to form the base of an all-green wreath decorated with dried hops, dried hydrangea florets and the green form of love-lies-bleeding.

Doubling, or tripling, as here, the number of wall rings provides an opportunity for long-term growth. Like the add-a-pearl necklaces that were once more popular than they are now, the wall display can be enlarged gradually, as and when you wish. If you are just beginning to work with dried flowers, it is less daunting to attempt a small project and repeat it several times than attempt one large one.

These three little rings are made of helichrysum heads fixed with quick-drying glue onto circular bases of cardboard tubing wrapped with green tape. Equally suitable are florists' foam rings. The matching tree is made the same way, using a tape-wrapped polystyrene ball. Modest without being uninteresting, and feminine without being coy, this combination of rings and tree would suit a girl's bedroom, or a flowery living room. The flowers are used in mixed shades of pink, cream, orange and red, but the rings could be colour-coded instead, each one a different shade, to pick up furnishing colours.

Helichrysums are one of the least expensive flowers available; more exotic material of the same scale includes heads of dried roses or bauble-like craspedia; silvery-blue echinops and sea holly; and small French marigolds. Whatever the main ingredient, the overall effect could be softened by interspersing sprigs of dried gypsophila, sea lavender or dill.

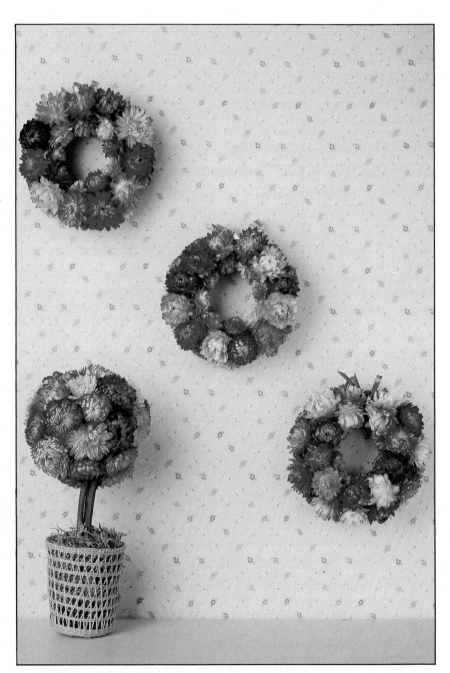

Trellis work, whether old-fashioned wood or plastic-coated wire, is a common garden feature, but it can form the basis of a permanently blooming indoor garden as well. Use the trellis like an empty canvas, on which to build up a painting in dried flowers. The size can range from quite small panels, such as the wooden trellis shown, to huge, ceiling-height panels, complete with arches and false perspective.

Shades of blue, grey-green and white form the colour theme of this wall hanging. Small bunches containing white, blue or grey-green flowers or foliage – white delphiniums, blue statice and grey-green grass, for example – are wired into triple bunches, then wired onto the trellis work and tied at the back. It is developed from the top of the trellis down, so that each little bouquet hides the stems and wiring of the bouquet above it. Tight bunches of lavender are used on their own, and large clusters of love-in-a-mist seed heads are worked through the arrangement to fill in any gaps at the end, and make a central focal point.

Dyed dried flowers have a dubious reputation in the floral world, partly due to the way they are used – or misused, as the case may be. The harsh dyed colours in strictly formal arrangements can look very unnatural. When dyed and non-dyed dried material are mixed, the intensity of the former can make the subtle colouring of the latter look dull, if not dirty. Then, too, some people have a philosophical prejudice against dyed material,

automatically putting it on the same level of kitsch as plastic flowers or those made out of old nylon stockings. In fact, like most other raw materials, dyed dried flowers can be used successfully.

The sea holly in this arrangement is dyed a steely deep blue, and, interestingly, it is the silvery-white stems, rather than the near-black seed heads, that benefit most. The dye gives the stems a beautiful

incandescent blue sheen, and the lower, thicker stems, which are normally discarded during the course of developing an arrangement, become a main feature. Although probably considered sacrilege in traditional schools of thought, some of the more delicate stems have their terminal flowers removed altogether, and their delicate tracery is used as a contrast to the dense build up .

Large-Scale Arrangements

There are no minimum measurements which define a large-scale arrangement, and on the whole, large-scale arrangements are governed by the same design guidelines as ordinary-sized displays. The finished effect, however, should be one of overwhelming abundance, with perhaps a hint of the theatrical.

The staging of large-scale displays is important to maximize the sense of scale. A big arrangement displayed in a narrow entrance hall will seem larger than that same arrangement dwarfed in a huge room. Although few homes have niches, which are ideal settings for large-scale floral displays, placing a huge dried flower arrangement in the corner of a room does make the arrangement seem larger. Placing an arrangement in front of a mirror has the effect of adding space to the room, and size to the arrangement, as long as the arrangement virtually touches the mirror, so that the arrangement and its reflection are continuous. Otherwise, the mirror will simply reflect the back of the arrangement, which is usually the least attractive view.

Although two of the three displays shown (pages 64 and 65) are photographed next to chairs, to give a sense of comparative scale, in real life, large-scale arrangements should have space round them. They can then be seen and admired without visual interruption, and are also less likely to get knocked or damaged.

Because large-scale arrangements usually require masses of dried material, it is tempting to try to fit in as many different varieties as possible. Although there are exceptions, this often leads to a bitty, fragmented finished effect. It is generally more effective to limit the range of material, and use massed bunches of single types of flowers or seed heads, rather like painting a huge canvas with broad brush strokes.

The natural affinity of dried flowers and wicker-work results in endless, pleasant flower-filled baskets; what makes this one memorable is the scale of the display. Over 75cm (30in) across, the basket holds hundreds of flowers; it is intended to impress and succeeds.

One key to this success is the wire mesh foundation, which is mounded above the rim of the basket. Rather like tiered seating in a theatre, no flowers obscure those behind them, although all are of similar height.

The flowers, on natural stems, are used in small bunches, for ease of construction and for visual coherence. The same number of flowers used singly would read like tiny specks on an all-over patterned wallpaper. The arrangement is built up gradually, so that it develops with equal density. Starting at one corner, filling it completely and working slowly across the area to be covered, is a more rigid approach and the finished display is liable to look contrived.

The flowers consist largely of 'old friends'; helichrysum, achillea, gypsophila, delphinium, lady's mantle, echinops, sea lavender and helipterum. The bell-shaped green bracts of Bells of Ireland stand out from among the rest. Glycerined, the bracts turn a pale, creamy white; air-dried, they retain much of their green colouring, though they eventually fade, and tend to drop.

Because this arrangement depends on such a huge array of different flowers, suggesting individual substitutes would be a pointless exercise. Unless the flowers are home grown and dried, it would be equally pointless attempting to do the display on a shoestring budget. No dyed flowers are used, and although some, such as dyed pink anaphalis, could be safely introduced. Dyed flowers of many different colours, or of strident colours, would mar the lovely, straight-from-the-garden effect.

This scale, approach and choice of flowers would be suitable for a display in a fireplace. Fill the grate with wire mesh and proceed as above, concealing any wire visible between the slats with more flowers.

Containers designed for purely functional purposes often have a special charm when used as part of a decorative floral display. The Victorian jelly mould shown on page xxx is a small example; this stainless steel milk churn is a large one. On a more pragmatic level, containers without aspirations to being art are usually less expensive, and often more attractive, than those of similar size and of materials which are heavily decorated.

The milk churn is packed three-quarters full with tightly crumpled newspaper before the flowers are inserted. Most of the dried material is used in its original bunches, as bought or dried. The tied bunches are easier to handle, and the string is ultimately concealed, either in the churn, or by overlapping flowers. The bleached wheat is used singly to add lightness to the display, and the single ornamental onion seed head is large enough not to need repetition.

The flowers are built up in layers, starting with the love-in-a-mist, and depend on compression rather than insertion into wire mesh or florists' foam, for stability. The stems of the lavender bunches, for example, are wedged firmly between bunches of love-in-a-mist, so that the lavender stems don't actually reach the container. This highly unconventional approach is perfectly adequate if the arrangement is built *in situ*. The traditional technique of wiring each bunch of lavender to a stout wire, long enough to act as an extended stem and reach well into the churn, would be sensible if the arrangement needed to be moved from one place to another, or if it were particularly vulnerable to disturbance.

Bunches of beige broom bloom are added last, to form a delicate collar which conceals the poker-straight stems of the love-in-a-mist. The broom bloom also helps soften the awkwardness of a wide flower arrangement growing out of a narrow-necked container.

The farming imagery of the milk churn immediately suggests an alternative arrangement, made up of dried material collected from roadsides and hedgerows; wild grasses, teasels, thistles, cow parsley heads and rich, red-brown dock seed heads. Although beautiful when dried, which it does naturally, dock is also a prolific garden weed. Care should be taken that none of the seed falls in the garden on the way to the house!

Large-scale arrangements needn't be expensive, as this elegant 'cherry blossom' tree proves. Less than one bunch of dried pink delphinium was used in its construction. The framework is made of several catkin-covered hazel branches inserted into a base of florists' foam; quick-setting plaster could also be used. The top surface in the container is a layer of sphagnum moss, as is the tiny nest perched in the branches and discreetly wired for stability. Speckled quail eggs complete the spring image; these are available from larger supermarkets and should be blown if the display is to be permanent.

The most costly component is the garlanded terra cotta pot, but even this is a modern replica and not exorbitantly expensive. It also lasts a lifetime, and most people would find it more attractive than its plastic equivalents. In practical terms, the terracotta provides weight and therefore stability to an otherwise vulnerable display.

Once the tree is built, the tiny delphinium flowers, or florets, are attached to the branches, using quick-drying glue. It is better to distribute them evenly over the tree, and build up a density gradually, than to thickly cover one branch and then go on to the next one. The florets are easier to glue to the point where one branch meets another than along an open branch.

The possible variations on this theme are enormous; a traditional wooden Versailles tub, either black or white; a simple, undecorated terracotta flower pot, perhaps spray-painted to match the flowers;

concrete pots, made to look like old stone; fibreglass containers, made to look like lead; and attractively glazed Chinese pots, all of which are available from larger garden centres. Glazed, decorated indoor containers, such as an old chamber pot, a huge cache pot or soup tureen; and wicker containers, such as a large laundry or log basket, are possibilities, as no watering or drainage holes are necessary.

Flowers could be of mixed colours of a single species – white and pink helipterum, for example – even mixed species. There is a precedent for this, in that branches of different varieties of Japanese cherry trees are occasionally grafted onto a single trunk, to produce a multicoloured, surreal floral display.

Any nicely shaped branches, or even a whole shrub or small tree, can be used instead of hazel branches.

Purist Arrangements

This category isn't found in conventional books on flower arranging, although there are many examples of such arrangements illustrated in contemporary interior design magazines and catalogues. The technique involves using relatively few floral ingredients to create an uncluttered display of simple shape. A dozen poppy seed heads in a plain glass tumbler is a purist arrangement in its most basic form. To some people, such a design is too simple and easy to be valid and doesn't really count as flower arranging, in rather the same way that, to some people, modern abstract paintings don't qualify as art. Other people feel that purist arrangements allow the flowers, whether fresh or dried, to be shown off to their fullest, without artificiality or distraction. Again, it is a matter of personal taste, although extreme purist arrangements, stripped down to the absolute minimum, can seem totally anonymous.

Such arrangements require simple containers, which don't detract from the colour or form of the floral material. Unfussy shapes, such as glass or ceramic cylinders, cubes or spheres, are the usual choices, as are plain colours.

The settings in which the following purist arrangements were photographed are designed to display the flowers at their best, and not compete with them. Like the settings used in food photography, a bit of poetic license is called for and, indeed, necessary. Purist arrangements in an equally stripped-down domestic setting – dried white gypsophila in a white vase displayed against a plain white wall, for example – can be equally dramatic, if well lit and generously proportioned. But they can also smack of cowardice, as if dealing with colour or revealing any hint of personal taste is too frightening a prospect altogether. A good and easy compromise – a more humanistic approach – is to place a purist arrangement in front of a landscape painting or poster; or even in front of a window looking out over a garden. Perhaps a bit less detail is visible and the silhouette of the arrangement may be slightly obscured, but the backdrop adds a softening, even humorous touch.

Blue Bowl with Seed Pods

This arrangement has an interesting history, having started life in the Victorian cache pot shown on page 42. Although an attractive combination in themselves, the balloon-like love-in-a-mist seed pods, spikes of chenopodium and delicate infill of lady's mantle looked out of place in the cache pot. This may have been because the dried material had a feeling of airy lightness, when a feeling of weight was called for, or because the dried seed pods and flowers looked too modern in such an old-fashioned container.

For whatever reason, several people, each with a different sense of style and taste, voiced disapproval. The arrangement, complete with its wire-mesh base, was then moved to the simple and more compatible blue earthenware bowl. The bowl is slightly shallower than the cache pot, so the small amount of wire visible is concealed by a collar of sphagnum moss packed round the base. The lesson to be learned is that experimentation, even at a late stage, can often lead to an improved finished article.

Love-in-a-mist is immensely useful in dried flower arranging, because of its chameleon-like quality. The bloated, often striped seed pods can appear strikingly modern, as here, or delicately old-fashioned, when combined with more traditional dried flowers.

Love-in-a-mist is also an inexpensive filler and its grey-green leaf-like colour is useful for cooling down the harsher hues of some dried flowers – statice and helichrysum, for example. Its own lacy foliage, to which 'mist' refers, is sparse. There are two more bonuses to be had from this jack-of-all-trades; occasionally, seed pods still have petals of the clearest blue adhering to them, and the tiny black seeds that sometimes spill out can be scattered in the garden.

Honesty seed pods dried while still green could be substituted for love-in-a-mist, although their two-dimensional flatness makes them less useful as a filler. Grasses, such as fescue, lesser quaking grass or phragmites, could be substituted for the spiky chenopodium, and sprigs of dried cress, used in place of the lady's mantle.

A traditional, white china soufflé dish, French enamelled cast iron pot or moss-lined glass bowl would make equally suitable containers.

Glass Battery Jar

The cloud of white flowers, floating above a Victorian glass battery jar, is a typical purist arrangement. The shapes – one broadly vertical, the other broadly horizontal – are simple, and the ingredients, few, but the finished effect is striking.

The sphagnum moss filling the glass is only 2.5cm (1in) thick. Behind it, the bulk of the filling is florists' foam. As the arrangement is front facing, there is no need for a sphagnum moss lining on the rear vertical side. The florist's foam stops 15cm (6in) below the rim and the resulting shallow nest contains the natural flower stems, which are held in place by compression alone. The flowers – yellow-centred helipterum and ammobium, dill and gypsophila – are used in large bunches, and create a richly patterned, intricate, coral-like surface.

The two parallel white ribbons were an afterthought, but one which improved the proportion of the arrangement by visually reducing its height in relation to its width, and by integrating the colours.

Although dried flowers by their very nature tend to be permanent features, it would be very easy to remove the summery white flowers and replace them with another selection, perhaps an autumnal one based on Chinese lanterns, yellow roses and sweetcorn, leaving the mossy base intact as a permanent foundation. The ribbons could also be changed to match the flower colours, as they are held in place only by small strips of double-sided cellophane tape.

An unusual alternative would be to fill the space between the florist's foam and glass with a thin layer of potpourri, either a single type or stripes of several different colours. A 'tree' of bare branches, such as birch, could be inserted into the florists' foam, and more potpourri used to cover the surface.

Glass marbles or gravel chippings could be used to line the container. Several natural fillers could be used in layers, like a geological section. Larger pebbles, peat, larch or small pine cones, wood chippings and attractive sections of bark could be included, as well as layers of sphagnum, bun and reindeer moss. The more varied and complicated the materials lining the container, the simpler the flower display should be, to avoid visual confusion.

For Christmas, the glass container could be filled with silver Christmas tree balls, topped with huge bunches of dyed craspedia, with its bright red baubles, and dyed red broom bloom. Neither of these dried flowers is particularly natural looking, but they combine well with the high sheen and artificiality of the metallic Christmas tree balls.

Brass Shell Case

This display, with its Oriental overtones, is based on a wider range of dried material than the other purist examples shown, but is included here for its low-key colours, its combination of unusual material, and its feeling of serenity. There is little point in being pedantic about categorizing flower arrangements, except perhaps those entered in competitions. Like mixed-breed dogs and cats, flower arrangements that combine more than one style or stray from rigid principles can be extremely charming.

Alder branches, festooned with male catkins and female cones, form the backbone of the display, together with the poker-straight lesser reedmace, a smaller and more manageable relative of the giant cat-tail. The alder and reedmace are positioned first, to establish the general height and spread of the arrangement, and their cut ends are inserted firmly into florists' foam. The modest but always useful green spikes of chenopodium are inserted next, to create a filigree-like fan of background colour.

The wired-up fluffy seed heads of wild clematis add softness, and a cluster of browny black rudbeckia heads, Sweet Williams and chive flowers form the heart of the arrangement. The Sweet Williams are on their natural stems, and the chives are wired, but the wires are hidden inside their own hollow natural stems. This is a useful trick, although the concealed wire may be less flexible than taped wire. As well as many grasses, other suitable hollow or soft-pithed stems for using in this way include those of columbine, scabious, hydrangea, delphinium, dahlia, poppy and *Iris sibirica*.

Branches of hazel, and particularly the corkscrew hazel, could replace the alder; and the green, leafless branches of broom, the chenopodium. Stalks of bamboo, such as the white-and-green-variegated dwarf sasa, would be an attractive addition, perhaps instead of the reedmace, and would reinforce the Oriental quality of the display.

A single page of text attempting to explain what is a highly developed art form and lifelong commitment to its serious followers, is bound to fall short of the whole truth. Ikebana is the classic Japanese art of flower arranging, based upon the six Buddhist principles of wisdom; energy; concentration; patience; morality and generosity. Ikebana, or the 'path' or 'way' of flowers, was introduced, with Buddhism, to Japan in the sixth century, and was originally practiced by priests in the Buddhist temples. It is also based on *shibuii,* the principle of using the minimum amount of material, with total restraint, to create the maximum amount of beauty. More complex, and perhaps harder to attain in a Western culture, are the philosophical and emotional states – *furyu* – that the practice of ikebana is intended to encourage. These involve a rejection of worldy pursuits, an appreciation of imperfection as a higher state of perfection, and achieving serenity through a progressive series of emotional states – *sabi, wabi, aware* and *yugen.*

The two classic styles of Ikebana are *rikka* and *shoka,* also called *seika,* or *tenchijin.* The former follows the style originally used in the ancient Buddhist temples; enormous, vertical arrangements in ceremonial bronze containers. The latter style, derived from the former, is smaller scale and is based on an asymmetrical triangle, the three points of which are meant to symbolize heaven, man and earth. Great emphasis is placed on line. The traditional angle of the tallest

line, or *shin,* symbolising heaven, is 80 degrees; that of man, or *soe,* the intermediate line, 45 degrees; and the shortest material, symbolising earth, or *tai,* 15 degrees. Proportions are also determined traditionally; the height of the tallest material should be at least one and a half times the height of the container; the intermediate material two thirds of the height of the tallest; and the shortest material two thirds the height of the intermediate. There are formal, semi-formal and informal sub-styles of *shoka.*

Simpler and less formal is the *nageire,* or thrown in style. Its vertical arrangements are casual looking, but quite difficult to construct, based on interlocking branches. *Moribana,* or massed-flower style, is also relatively simple, with asymmetrical, naturalistic landscape-like or purely floral arrangements.

The arrangement shown is the abstract, or free style, a relatively recent development in Ikebana. It adheres to no formal rules and allows free self expression, but, like classical Ikebana, depends on a sense of balance, simplicity and restraint for its effect. Though free-form arrangements can contain such non-floral material as glass, feathers and painted branches, this one uses only natural material; larch branches, pressed ferns, seed head of field rape, poppy and grape hyacinth, and a single dried hydragea head.

The larch branches are inserted first into a small block of florists' foam, to establish height and a sense of movement. The three ferns are added next, then the grape hyacinth

and field rape to reinforce a sense of direction and lead the eye to the focal point, the cluster of poppy seed heads and hydrangea blossom.

Suitable alternative material could include dried bamboo leaves, lotus seed pods, broom branches twisted when fresh into the required shape then allowed to dry; and lesser reed mace. Traditionally, material is used according to season, and flowers that bloom naturally in winter, for example, are never combined with forced spring flowers. Although dried material has unlimited possibilities, you may wish to confine your choice to those that bloom in a single season.

Obviously, this rather austere style demands a simple container, such as the traditional Japanese one illustrated. Many department stores and florists import these, as well as the similar Japanese 'bonsai' containers. Other suitable ones are clear glass bowls or jars, plain brass or copper, or even simple ceramics. Avoid using painted china or very elaborate shapes, as these will detract from the clean, pure lines of the arrangement.

Table and Small Arrangements

This subject covers a multitude of possibilities, with a minimum of hard rules. There are, however, a few guidelines worth bearing in mind. Whatever the type of dried flowers used or the style of arranging, the size of the arrangement should be related to the size of the furniture surface on which it is displayed. A huge dried flower display that overspills its table base is liable to look odd as well as being unstable. A tiny arrangement on a vast tabletop, on the other hand, is liable to be overlooked completely, although a collection of tiny arrangements on a large table often has more visual impact than the sum of its parts.

Because dried flowers are by their nature fragile, they should be sited in the middle of a table or, at least, well away from where they are in danger of being knocked over. And because they are lightweight, dried flowers in a lightweight container are particularly vulnerable. Weighting the container with pebbles, marbles or even sand is a sensible precaution, if the table is near the normal flow of family traffic.

Dried flowers on the dining table, whether as a centrepiece or as individual arrangements at each place setting, should never impede comfortable dining or conversation. Huge, sprawling arrangements that encroach upon the food or obstruct the view of other diners are unsuitable, however magnificent the arrangement may be in itself. A huge dried flower arrangement on a coffee table between two facing sofas can be similarly obstructive, and a low, spreading one might be more suitable.

Small arrangements should be placed where they can be seen up close, and perhaps even picked up and admired in detail. If there are young children in the house, however, access to dried flower arrangements should be strictly, if temporarily, limited.

Whatever the size of the arrangement, make sure that the container is not liable to scratch or otherwise damage the surface of the furniture. A tablecloth or lace-edged doily, with a place mat underneath, if necessary, is a pretty and practical solution. If you are using a flat-based container and want no visual interruptions, trace the bottom of the container onto a thin piece of card or fabric, such as felt, cut it out and place it underneath the container.

Some popular flowers are so well known that they become stereotyped and tend to be used only in traditional ways; the tall spikes of delphiniums to add height to an arrangement, and the airy white sprays of gypsophila to add mass, for example. If, on the other hand, flowers are seen simply as raw material, to be experimented with and perhaps even taken apart, the resulting arrangements are likely to have more originality and flair.

The dried flowers – technically florets – of pink delphinium and pale stems of gypsophila are combined in an unexpected way in the feminine bedside-table tree illustrated. A wooden dowel is the usual choice for a miniature standard tree trunk, and is adequate for the purpose, but the thick stems of dried gypsophila provide a more natural-looking alternative, complete with branches. Other possibilities from nature include suitably scaled-down tree branches and twigs, and the thick stems of such herbaceous plants as honesty, perennial rudbeckia, kangaroo paw, teasel and hogweed.

The trunk is inserted well into florists' foam held in position on a frog attached to mastic. The top of the foam is concealed by sphagnum moss. An alternative is to fill the base with quick-setting plaster. Allow time to dry, before covering the base with bun moss or reindeer moss. Small pebbles can also be pressed into the wet plaster to give a rough stone effect. For an all-pink scheme, use a layer of pink helipterum or globe amaranth.

The top of the trunk is inserted into a florists' foam ball and groups

of three or four delphinium florets, and occasional green flower buds, are wired together to form tightly packed bunches. The wires are then pushed into the ball, evenly building up the flowers, until the surface becomes a dense mass of colour.

Resting dried delphinium florets round the base of a candle holder is

a nice finishing touch, but in terms of home safety, the candle should be a non-drip one, or else remain unlit. Spraying the basket a toning matt pink is another pretty touch, although many people find the neutral colour of wickerwork is equally pleasing.

Dried flowers displayed in or on sea shells make a natural twosome, with their complementary organic forms. (The Victorians, in their creative enthusiasm, used tiny sea shells to make artificial flowers, a craft still carried on in some seaside resorts.) Many shells are subtly and beautifully coloured, and repeating their colour or colour combinations with dried flowers can be very successful.

As well as the pleasurable pastime of collecting the shells by the sea, there are specialist shops that sell shells, and some tropical aquarium suppliers also carry a range of unusual shells, intended for fish tank decorations but equally useful for the flower arranger. Lastly, many fish shops have oysters, scallops and other molluscs 'on the shell'; these shells, once empty and thoroughly washed, make excellent bases for small-scale dried flower arrangements.

In the multiple display (right), the delicately beaded sea urchin shell provides the base for an all-white dried flower arrangement. Sprigs of unwired statice, and wired-up dill and gypsophila are inserted into a small block of florists' foam, attached to a frog and mastic on the top of the shell. The theme is continued in miniature in the small cockle shells; tiny sprigs of mixed flowers are wired together and the wire inserted directly into florists' foam.

An alternative, but equally attractive, combination would be sprigs of white sea lavender, pink delphinium florets and pink campion filling the glossy pink aperture of a conch shell. Tiny whelk or cowrie shells could be substituted

for the cockle shells, to complete the 'mother and babies' theme.

The scallop shell (far right) contains a mixture of pastel-coloured helichrysums, xeranthemum, goldenrod and various seed heads; the strikingly dark rudbeckia seed heads contrast with the pastels and keep the display from becoming saccharine. The flowers are fixed into a small cube of florists' foam

fixed with quick-drying glue onto the shell.

The high gloss of the wooden table reflects in detail the underside of the scallop shell, as an additional bonus. Ormers, or sea ears, with their thick inner layer of mother of pearl, would make lovely alternative containers; very large ormer shells can occasionally be had, for more dramatic displays.

Dried flower arrangements for individual place settings should be approached with a sense of adventure, but also one of caution. If the table is crowded with cutlery, china and glassware, then a single, central arrangement is more sensible. This is also true if the table is set for a children's party, where over-exuberance is likely to overcome good manners. However, for a leisurely luncheon for two or a dinner party where there is plenty of space, individual arrangements, either on their own, or mirroring in miniature a central floral display, add to the spirit of the occasion.

China sets which have matching egg cups offer ready made containers, but any plain china or wooden egg cups can be used. Flat-bottomed egg cups are more stable than stemmed ones, an important point since dried flowers have so little weight. Most egg cups can accommodate a single frog attached to mastic; pack very small egg cups with florists' foam, until it is wedged tightly in position. Old-fashioned demi-tasse cups are also suitable, though these are harder to find.

The tiny flower arrangement mirrors the informality and colour scheme of the white-glazed stoneware and hessian cloth setting. The phalaris seed heads, white statice, yellow lady's mantle and sprigs of beige butcher's broom are offset by the unusual, wine-red helichrysums.

Fresh flowers are often floated or rested in wine glasses, one at each setting, but the basically unattractive stems of dried flowers need concealing. Try making a small,

central arrangement, then fill the wine glass with pebbles, clear glass marbles or line it with sphagnum moss, for a pretty effect; the pebbles and marbles also add stability. Wine glasses can also be filled with potpourri, on its own or as a fragrant camouflage for the stems of a miniature dried flower bouquet.

Wine glasses can be filled with dry salt, then short-stemmed dried flowers inserted. Another alternative is to line the wine glasses with silver foil. Make a small posy of dried flowers, a little wider than the top of the glass. Place a paper doily round the posy and tie the stems. Cut the stems short, then insert in the glass.

Props are used boldly and without shame in theatre production, gallery and museum exhibitions and in shop window displays. With flower arranging, however, the word props conjures up heavily draped velvet backdrops, coy figurines in court dress, formal candelabra and perhaps even convoluted bits of driftwood, included to add mood or movement to a formal arrangement. While any of these props might be successfully used to enhance an arrangement, their predictability usually makes for an unmemorable finished effect.

There is, however, no need to entirely dismiss the use of props simply because some are over-used, or insensitively used. An ordinary home contains a wealth of unusual props, ready for the taking, to add charm and individuality to even the most modest floral display. The arrangement shown is based on a small bunch of mixed statice, one of the least expensive and easily available dried flowers. It is given an unexpected sense of drama and humour by the nearby presence of a glazed ceramic sheep – in fact, a child's piggy bank, borrowed for the occasion. The theme of white on white is continued in the Victorian glazed and woven cache-pot, so that the soft colours of the statice are displayed without competition.

In practical terms, the sides of the cache-pot should be lined with black or dark green polythene taped into position. The statice stems are inserted into florist's foam which is held in position by a frog attached to mastic.

Moss Garden

Miniature moss gardens are as charming as they are easy to make, and are ideal projects for children. Miniature moss gardens often feature in the children's section of country flower shows and fêtes. Though the finished effect is one of lush opulence, miniature moss gardens are in fact quite economical to construct, and require a minimum of dried flowers. For the economy minded, moss gardens are perfect for making use of the odd dried flower head that has come adrift from its stem. Moss gardens are attractive all year round, but are particularly welcome in winter, when they offer a contrast in miniature to the usually bleak garden scene outside.

Moss, the main component, can either be fresh or dried. Dried mosses include the thread-like sphagnum moss, silvery grey bun moss, various selaginellas and the creamy white reindeer moss (technically a lichen). Fresh moss, creates an incredibly verdant effect, and should remain fresh for several weeks in a cool room. If you are using fresh moss, check for small creatures and scrape off most of the soil from the underside before you start, to avoid a messy end result.

Choose a container, keeping in mind the amount of material you have, where the display is to go, and the likely attention span, if it is a child's project. A teacup saucer is a sensible choice for a very young child. Shallow containers are most often used, but you could use a deeper one, tightly packing it first with crumpled newspaper or dry florist's foam, nearly up to the rim. If

woven or otherwise perforated, first line the container with black or dark green polythene taped to the sides. With rimless bases, such as wooden bread boards or marble cheese slabs, fix the moss to florist's foam held in position with frogs and mastic. Using wires bent to a hairpin shape; thick clumps of bun moss can be fixed directly onto frogs.

Decide whether the garden is to be viewed in the round or from the front only, before you start. Tightly pack the moss, so that no florist's foam, plastic lining or container is visible. Gentle level changes can be made by building up the moss in layers. Two-tiered gardens, such as the one illustrated, are made by using a rectangular block of florist's foam, fixed through the base with reel wire or held in position on frogs and mastic, in the case of solid containers. Irregularly shaped florist's foam can be used as the foundation for miniature mountains and gorges.

When the moss is in position, begin placing the larger features in the landscape; pebbles or sea-washed stones; lichen-covered sections of bark or lengths of wood; and 'trees' of twigs, such as alder, sea lavender, or gypsophila stems. Insert dried flowers, singly or in clumps, as you build up the scene. Flowers that are out of scale will instantly declare themselves, so be prepared to experiment. It is sometimes a case of simply choosing a smaller bloom of that variety, or of dividing a bigger flower, such as achillea, into individual florets, and occasionally of admitting defeat and choosing a different variety altogether.

Potpourri Tray

A little potpourri can be made to go a long way, in terms of visual impact and fragrance. A very effective and economical trick-of-the-trade is to use potpourri one layer thick, that is, only as thick as is necessary to hide the filler beneath it. The latter can be florist's foam, sphagnum moss or tissue paper.

If using tissue paper, scrunch it up tightly and work it well into the corners of the container, so that the base of the final layer of potpourri is compact and level on the surface. Otherwise, the precious petals will disappear into corners and interstices, and retrieving them is a maddening exercise.

Potpourri, particularly that composed entirely of petals, tends to appear two dimensional, rather like textured fabric. While there is nothing wrong with this and rainbow-like layers of different potpourris can be quite beautiful, combining potpourri with ordinary dried flowers gives greater scope for creativity, and the end result has a more three-dimensional presence. The dried flowers can repeat those contained in the potpourri, or be quite different; whatever looks nice is right.

The mixed display illustrated is based on a humble woven cutlery tray, with each compartment holding a different potpourri. An asymmetrical focal point is formed by a bunch of anaphalis edged with red rose buds. The anaphalis is dyed, as is obvious from its pink-tinged, slightly wild leaves, but the colour is pleasing, and the only possible objection could be a philosophical one.

Gifts and Miniatures

Dried flowers provide a wealth of raw material for gifts and, unlike fresh flowers, dried flowers continue to give pleasure long after they are given. Some people enjoy flower arranging, and would frankly prefer to be given a generous bunch of dried flowers. Left to get on with it, they then have the choice of doing one large arrangement or several small ones, each to match a specific decor or position. Other people would much prefer a finished product, ready for instant display, without any personal input. The closer you can match your dried flower gift to the creativity level of its recipient, the better its reception will be. Other matching considerations include the colour likes and dislikes of the recipient, and, if it is a finished arrangement, whether its formality or informality is likely to match the style of the decor. All of this assumes you know the person well, which may not be the case. You can rest assured, though, that a gift of mixed dried flowers, especially in neutral or soft colours, is always welcome.

As far as the size of the gift goes, a small miniature flower arrangement can convey the spirit of generosity just as much as a larger one. Ironically, it is often the tiny arrangements that take a lot of time to make, because each component – each twig, flower head or even bud – is in full view, and therefore must be flawless in itself and beautifully placed in relation to the whole. In practical terms, small arrangements and miniatures are particularly appreciated by children, who like to be surrounded by possessions scaled down to their own size; and by people living in small flats or otherwise cramped accommodation. Then, too, some people are natural 'squirrels', intent on filling their domestic 'nests' with collections of tiny trinkets. Whatever the size of their homes, such people are always delighted with miniature gifts, which offer the challenge of incorporating them into already crowded display cases or shelves, and the excuse to rearrange their existing possessions.

Years ago, fresh flowers were *de rigueur* at formal occasions, usually worn pinned to the dress, but sometimes as a wrist corsage or, more daringly, in the hair. This practice extended to less formal occasions, such as first dates and school dances. The corsages were short lived, but still valued for their fleeting beauty and their romantic symbolism. The dried flower earrings shown are fragile, but just as romantic and, if treated carefully, longer lived. Kept for special occasions, and stored in a dark place, they should last for six or more wearings. A word of warning; they are not particularly compatible with disco dancing, wet weather or certain hair styles.

Because of the natural variation in dried flowers, a pair of earrings will never be identical. Trying to get them to match perfectly can be frustrating and counter-productive, as the more the material is handled and fussed over, the more liable it is to break. It is better to accept the slight variations as part of the charm. Those shown are for pierced ears, but they could be adapted for non-pierced ears. Both types of earring pieces are available from craft shops.

Easiest to make are single-flower earrings, such as the wine-red helichrysums shown, fixed to the earring piece with a dab of clear, quick-drying glue. The yellow chrysanthemum heads are pierced with silver wire, then a single drop pearl is threaded onto the wire, which is looped back through the flower and fixed to the earring base.

For the bow and flower earrings, tiny bunches of broom bloom are

wired to silver wire which is then twisted round the earring piece. The little satin ribbons are tied on last.

Each bunch of white dill is also wired, and the wire is pushed through the hole of the white plastic bead, then wrapped round the earring piece.

More difficult are the long hanging earrings, built up of alternating flowers; pink delphinium and cream broom bloom; and blue cornflowers, cream broom bloom and lady's mantle. The flowers are wired onto

commercially available earring drops, from bottom upwards, using one long silver wire, which is then hooked onto the earring piece.

Hair grips and combs, small brooches or a drop for a necklace could be made in a similar way; but bracelets would probably not stand up to natural wear and tear. Miniature roses and tiny sprigs of heather or lavender could be substituted for the flowers shown. Freshly dried lavender, with its fragrance, would be delightful.

This enchanting collection of Lilliputian arrangements is based on the assumption that small is beautiful and miniature, more beautiful still. The kiwi fruit is included to give an indication of scale. A steady hand, patience, a pair of small scissors and, possibly, tweezers prove invaluable tools for work of this sort.

'Largest' of all is the wall-hung doll's hat, decorated with tiny buds and florets wired round a central cluster of helichrysum. Silver wire inserted through the straw holds the flowers and wide satin ribbon in position. Each doll-sized basket – and the 'odd-man-out' egg cup – contains a different combination of flowers, arranged to suit the colour and shape of the particular container. The larger baskets can just about accommodate the standard mastic, frog and florist's foam sub-structure; the flowers in the tiny baskets are simply held in position by small pieces of mastic alone. They can also be set in quick-drying plaster. Particularly interesting are the white basket, which is a crocheted doily dipped in starch and dried over a glass, and the tiny basket with pleated lace edging glued to the rim.

Even more minute alternative containers include the traditional silver thimble, tiny sea shells, an upturned lid or a perfume bottle. Almost anything is possible, but whether the resulting microscopic arrangements are diminutively attractive or silly is a matter of personal taste.

Genuine Victorian bell jars, used originally to keep dust off the delicate displays within, are relatively valuable and rare. If you are lucky enough to own one, it makes an ideal outer container for dried flowers; not only are they protected from dust, but also accidental knocking. The glass bell jar also gives dried flowers a theatricality and visual importance.

As far as any floral arrangement can be said to be feminine or masculine, in these days of sexual equality, the arrangement illustrated is a more masculine one; muted, neutral colours; a tightly compacted over-all shape; non-frilly floral material, with an emphasis on the cones and seed heads; and a simple container. The latter is an early twentieth-century glazed ceramic jelly mould. Its classic shape makes it worthy of display in even the most elegant setting.

Technically, the mould is packed with florist's foam impaled on a frog attached to mastic in the base of the container. The silvery blue-grey seed heads of echinops are used in tight bunches, as are the fir cones. Both are wired up, as the former has weakish stems and the latter has none at all. The white statice, blue-grey poppy seed heads, nearly black rudbeckia heads and creamy pink helichrysum are used on their natural stems. The display is built up like a tapestry, with interwoven patches of colour and texture. Alternative material with muted colouring and a sculptural, masculine feel include the bloated seed heads of love-in-a-mist and the curious, salt-cellar-shaped lotus fruit.

Mini Bell Jars

Floral displays in miniature bell jars, like miniature moss gardens, are worthy of a place at school fêtes and fund-raising bazaars, especially considering how little outlay is needed. It is an ideal project for using up all the bits and bobs of flower heads that have parted from their stems, and even a single bunch of dried (preferably mixed) flowers goes a long, long way.

Choose the jars with care. Although there is a certain amount of ship-in-a-bottle manipulation, the wider the mouth of the jar, the easier the exercise. Avoid jars that are tall and slender, and obviously those that have numbers or writing embossed on the bottom, because the jars are displayed bottoms up. Facetted jars are particularly attractive, as are those with slightly tinted glass.

Paint the lid before starting, then attach a small frog to the inside, using mastic, then impale a small piece of florist's foam to the frog. Alternatively, use a spot of quick-drying glue. Place the upturned jar over the lid, to check that the florist's foam fits comfortably inside, with room to spare all the way round. Begin to insert flowers into the florist's foam, checking frequently for fit. Feed the flowers through the mouth, if it is narrower than the rest of the jar, by gently pressing them inwards; they will expand to fill the jar once inside. Hide any florist's foam visible with moss, then secure the lid.

Use short, squat jars right-way up. Fill with potpourri and a small bunch of dried flowers, concealing the threads of a screw top with glued-on moss or thin ribbons.

Whether a present to yourself or someone else, the selection shown encompasses easy and pleasing possibilities. Easiest of all is potpourri – it is too fiddly to arrange, except possibly in broad bands of colour (*see page 81*), and so the only choice is one of presentation. Somehow the crumpled brown paper bags that potpourri is often sold in don't rise to the spirit of gift giving. A transparent container allows the colour as well as the fragrance to be enjoyed; shown here are three options.

A glass, such as the brandy snifter shown, can be an inexpensive receptacle for the potpourri or the real gift, with the potpourri in a supporting role. The pyramid-shaped clear plastic gift box, available from specialist stores, contains a tiny amount of potpourri, topped with slightly more extravagant dried rose heads sitting on a bed of white delphinium florets. And lastly, a circle of tulle is gathered to form a potpourri bag, tied at the neck with thin ribbon and embellished with a cluster of tiny flowers. Tulle or fine net potpourri bags are excellent if you have a large number of small presents to give, or perhaps to make for a Christmas bazaar; they will scent a drawer or cupboard for many months.

There is nothing unusual about the concept of dried-flower lollipop trees, but they can be customized in various ways. Spraying the flower pot with high-gloss emulsion to match the arrangement is one; adding toning ribbons is another. Even the surface finish beneath the tree leaves room for improvisation. A sphagnum moss or wood chippings finish is an easy solution; you could also use reindeer moss, as in the base of the red tree. The latter has its own miniature flower garden, repeating the choice of flowers in the tree. If you have enough material, try covering the entire base with flowers, so that no moss is visible. The base of the blue tree has a gravel finish; the bamboo cane stem is set in plaster and, when nearly dry, gravel is gently pressed into the surface. Tightly packed ash or hornbeam keys with some fir cones, their stems inserted into florist's foam, make an even more unusual surface finish.

The flower-filled tea pot and cup and saucer are self explanatory and, like the potpourri-filled brandy snifter, can range from the cheap and cheerful to the extraordinarily expensive. The fierce yellow and orange of tansy, Chinese lanterns, dyer's saffron and mimosa would be perfect for the similarly coloured 'Thirties and 'Forties china.

Harvest Displays

More than for any other occasion, largesse is the key to a successful harvest display, whether for an American-style Thanksgiving dinner or a church festival. Grains and ornamental grasses, maize cobs, nuts and dried gourds are all part of the language of harvest, and the range of warm yellows, oranges, reds and browns which dried flowers and foliage offer is a perfect complement.

Size is a two-edged sword; a feeling of generosity can be conveyed on quite a small scale, and the reverse is also true. Given a modest amount of dried material, it is better to over-fill a small basket than to half-fill a large one.

The harvest season is also a time for swags and wreaths of dried material. A wreath, or candlestick rings, of tightly packed wired-up nuts can do duty in the autumn, then be sprayed silver or gold for Christmas. Bunches of dried maize, their dried husks still attached, are the traditional door decoration for an American Thanksgiving; other alternatives or additions to an autumnal door swag include dried artichoke heads; cereal grains and ornamental grasses; Chinese lantern branches, and teasel. Try ringing a mirror or picture frame with a rope of dried material with harvest overtones, or, if time and supplies allow, surround a whole window or door frame with a swag. Again, thickly braided raffia forms a useful base, which can be studded here and there or completely concealed with dried flowers and seed heads.

More generally autumnal than harvest orientated is the display of preserved foliage, seed heads, cones and dried flowers, on its purpose-made base of sawn oak. A piece of felt, cut out by using the base as a template, is glued to the bottom, to prevent scratching, and a block of florist's foam is wired to the wood.

The height and width of this roughly triangular arrangement is established first by the beech foliage. Infill consists of helichrysum, statice, pine cones, ferns, poppy, honesty, old man's beard and scabious seed heads, goldenrod, lady's mantle, laurel leaves, teasel, various grasses and the curiously spider-like leaf of the so-called stinking hellebore. Leafless branches of climbing bittersweet would make an attractive addition; pick before the orange outer calyx has opened to reveal the showy red seeds.

Harvest Basket

The harvest display shown is based on a huge basket, decorated first with two rows of braided raffia around the sides, and a row across the handle, tied on with single raffia strips. Strips of raffia are also used to attach bunches of happy flower to the handle. The basket is then filled nearly to the top with newspaper, well compacted to avoid subsidence, followed by a top layer of mixed sphagnum and reindeer mosses, to hide the newspaper.

Walnuts, hazel nuts, chestnuts, pecans and Brazil nuts can be polished, or sprayed with a proprietary glossy varnish to enrich their colour and make them shiny. When dry, they are piled, each according to type, on the moss bed. Three dried, varnished ornamental gourds form a large-scale focal point. Branches and single pods of Chinese lantern, together with clusters of dried grass, each according to kind and each bound with silver wire, fill the interstices. Finally, creamy white heads of helichrysum bring the basket almost to overflowing.

Including fresh grapes, apples, pears and arching blackberry branches or sprays of rose hips, or the more unusual quince and medlar, is the equivalent of including fresh flowers; fair game, with stunning but shorter lived, results possible.

The setting in this display is frankly a piece of artistic licence, and, in spite of its haphazard appearance, required almost as much arranging, and at least as much material, as the arrangement itself. Admittedly not possible on a domestic scale, this massive overflowing of a harvest display is very effective.

Easter Displays

Fresh flowers are part of the symbolism of Easter and it would be stretching credibility to suggest that dried flowers could ever replace Easter lilies. On a more secular level, Easter is a spring event, and the fresh daffodils, hyacinths, primroses, iris, violets and tulips that fill gardens and florists then are very tempting and valuable material for the flower arranger. That said, dried flowers still have much to offer in their own right.

Freshly cut pussy willow, like freshly cut broom, can be bent into a tight curve or other desired shape. Moisten it thoroughly, then use firm, but not rough, finger pressure; wire can also be used. Keep the shaped branch out of water until thoroughly dried. Other branches suitable for Easter displays include the angular, green and leafless stems of spindle berry, which, when combined with fresh lilies, visually symbolises the rebirth of spring and the Resurrection. Equally effective would be the twisted, silvery grey branches of wisteria or elegant branches of deciduous magnolia.

On a small scale, tiny dried flowers can be used to decorate blown and dyed eggs, perhaps in combination with narrow ribbons and lace. Use quick-drying glue, and remember always to save the bits and bobs of flowers that remain after creating a large arrangement; you will come to value them for mini-projects such as this one. Before starting, decide how the eggs are to be displayed. If in individual egg cups, decorate the tops only, but those displayed in 'nests' of hay, straw or moss, can be decorated along one side, if wished. If displayed in a shallow straw basket, work some of the ribbon through the weave of the basket, or tie it into tiny bows at regular intervals.

The centrepiece shown – a floral hen, sitting on a raffia nest and surrounded by little egg-filled Easter baskets – is a reference to the more light-hearted side of this festival, especially as seen from a child's point of view. The main framework is a bird-shaped wire salad shaker. Wire mesh formed into a bird shape could be used instead, or, on a smaller scale, a block of florist's foam can be carved into shape.

Filled with sphagnum moss, the wire framework provides a base for closely packed dried flowers in traditional yellow and white Easter colours. The short stalks are simply wedged between the rows of narrow, parallel wires. Helichrysum, acroclinium, achillea, lady's mantle, sprigs of broom bloom, happy flower used in tight clumps, statice, sunrays and dyed phalaris seed heads form the bulk of the bird's feathers, together with the velvet centres of leopard's bane, two of which form the eyes. Almost any non-spiky flowers could be substituted or added to this display, as the flowers are used *en masse.* It is an ideal project for using up flower heads that have come adrift from their stems, or less than perfect flower heads, as missing petals are unlikely to be noticed.

The tail is made of bleached agrostis and small sprigs of pampas grass. A few turkey or cockerel feathers could also be added. Pampas grass is readily available but the huge silky plumes are visually very dominant and can be difficult to use with other dried material; this is equally true of pampas grass in the garden. The plumes, however, can

be taken apart and the feather 'plumelets', each with a sturdy stalk, are far more useful, in this form, or wired onto longer stems. (The secret of preventing the plumes disintegrating into useless fluff is to harvest them in early autumn, when the seed heads open, but have not yet become fluffy.)

Oriental woven baskets are available in the shape of birds, and packing one with moss, then filling the middle with dried flowers, would be an easier Easter centrepiece to make. Although the connection between rabbits and eggs is

zoologically tenuous, Easter bunnies are an important part of this festivity for children, and a rabbit-shaped basket could be used.

Pussy willows are a lovely garden feature at this time of year, and combining masses of pussy willow with bunches of dried buttercups, pot marigolds or yellow rose buds would make a more sophisticated display. Daffodils can be dried in silica gel, but to produce a display, however beautiful, of desiccated daffodils at Easter goes against the spirit of the season and of flower arranging generally.

Christmas Displays

Dried flowers are not inherently part of the decorative symbolism of Christmas, although dried seed pods are a natural part of the winter scene in the temperate Northern Hemisphere. Pine and other conifer cones, technically seed pods, do have connotations of Christmas. Christmas trees go back at least to medieval Central Europe, and were made popular in Germany by Martin Luther. Queen Victoria and Prince Albert further popularized Christmas trees in England. The practice of adorning houses and churches with evergreen foliage – ivy, holm oak and bay, as well as conifers – at Christmas-time is far older, and probably has its origins in earlier religions.

Naturally dried flowers and foliage do not provide the pure, almost electric red and green that have come to be associated with Christmas, especially the manufactured decorations. The reds of dried helichrysum, dahlias, bottlebrush or cockscomb, for example, have a rich subtlety and variation, which can look odd seen against a piece of bright red felt or wrapping paper. Rich, bright green is simply not part of the palette of naturally dried material, and even fresh foliage can look motley compared to the dyed green of a tablecloth. Commercially dyed dried flowers and foliage can be had in bright red and green, although they sometimes lose in charm what they gain in colour intensity. The same can be true of material spray painted.

Dried material does have Christmas potential, but it needs careful thought. The following illustrations show how successful dried flowers, on their own or in combination with traditional evergreen foliage, can be. Their role can be conventional and high key, as in the dining table arrangement; or unusual and without artificial gloss, as in the Christmas wreath. Dried flowers and foliage can be treated as raw material, to be coloured and manipulated into fantastic shapes, or as finished objects in their own right, to be presented in a straightforward and pleasing way, with minimal touches of Christmas symbolism.

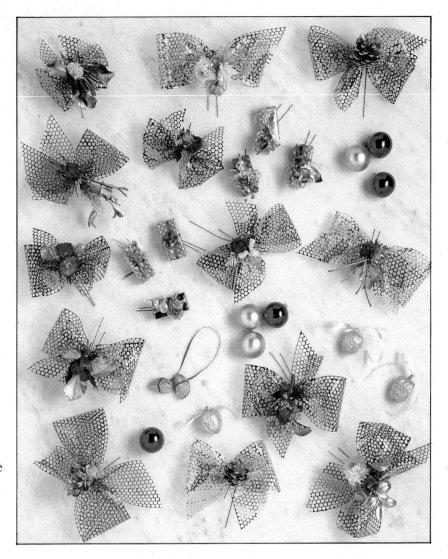

Christmas tree decorations depend on boldness and sheer numbers for impact, and also need to be visible from a distance. Dried material is delicate; and the smaller the scale, the plainer the background should be. These seemingly contradictory factors are happily resolved in the Christmas tree decorations shown. Dried material forms an integral part of each ornament, and stands up to close inspection, but there is enough glitter in the shiny bows and tiny, paper-wrapped chocolate boxes to be effective across the proverbial crowded room.

Tins of gold and silver spray paint are indispensable for instant transformation of non-Christmas material into potential Christmas tree decorations. The curious buds of dyer's greenwood; Chinese lantern seed pods; honesty seed pods; ash, hornbeam or sycamore seeds; flower-like beech mast; glycerined beech leaves; butcher's broom foliage; and alder branches are particularly effective when sprayed silver or gold. Anything that has a simple, sculptural shape is worth trying.

Although more expensive than ordinary paint, spray paint will get into the interstices of pine cones and teasel heads, and is delicate enough not to damage peeled honesty seed heads or rose or allium petals. Several light coats should be applied, to avoid the problem of unsightly dripping or congealing.

The simplest ornaments to make are those based on a bow and one central feature; a sprayed pine cone; cluster head of silver strawberries; or allium seed head, for example. The

feature is wired onto the bow, the wire also providing the means of attaching the ornament to the tree.

Wire little clusters of dried material together using silver wire, then attach them to the bow. Red roses and gold-sprayed beech leaves; a red rose, creamy white helichrysum and gold-sprayed box sprig; gold-sprayed alder catkins, gold-sprayed beech leaves and white statice; and silver-sprayed dyer's greenwood and gold-sprayed box foliage, are just a few of the combinations possible.

The same system works for the tiny, gift-wrapped chocolate boxes, except that the dried material should be diminutive; gold-sprayed sprigs of

broom bloom, a tiny beech leaf, a wisp of ornamental grass.

Pairs of sprayed nuts can be glued to thin ribbon. Sprayed walnuts can be drilled where the two halves meet at the top, fitted with tiny screw-in closed hooks and finished off with a ribbon bow and a loop of transparent nylon thread for hanging.

Not everyone has access to sequin waste for bows; wide satin ribbons in red, white, green, silver or gold could be substituted. Lengths of upholstery cord in similar colours could also be used. Prevent the two cut ends unravelling by knotting them, or securing with elastic bands, concealed with thin ribbons.

Some people expend all their creative energy in choosing Christmas presents, and the wrapping looks like the afterthought that it is. Other people enjoy planning and executing the presentation of a gift more than choosing it. Dried material can meet the needs of both these extremes, and the more usual range of attitudes in between.

All the gift boxes shown are self wrapped: that is, the decorative paper is part of the box and no additional paper is needed. Though more expensive, such boxes are attractive and make a sensible choice for the ham-handed. They also are slightly easier to decorate with dried flowers, as any wiring has to go through a single layer, not two.

Easiest of all is the gold-sprayed allium head – nature has done all the designing beforehand. Loop silver wire through the stemless head, then through a single hole in the box lid, and tape to the underside; or make two holes in the lid and twist the two ends of wire together on the underside.

Only a modest amount of work goes into the mini-bouquet on the gold box. A rose, gold-sprayed larch sprig and gold-sprayed honesty pods are wired together, then attached with wire to the white ribbon. The red box has a tiny bouquet of gold-sprayed beech leaves, helichrysum and hazel twigs, plus bright red craspedia heads, wired together and tied with a white bow. The bouquet is then wired to the pinched-in centre of a strip of sequin waste, and through the lid, as above.

The most time-consuming of all

are the three gold mini-boxes of chocolates, which decorate the gold and white gift box. Each mini-box is individually wrapped and tied, and a few sprigs of gold-sprayed broom bloom or grass seed heads are incorporated into the bow tie. Double-sided tape fixes the mini-boxes to the lid.

The glossy red paper gift bag has

all the virtues of ready-wrapped boxes. Matching reds can be a very tricky proposition, as can be seen from the several different red hues in the photograph. A posy of white dill and clematis seed heads is used instead, wired through the bag, then tied with a ribbon. A posy of gold- or silver-sprayed flowers would be equally effective.

others are sprayed lightly and some others, such as the orange helichrysum and neutral grasses, are left natural. The result is a glorious mixture of close-knit forms in a limited but interesting colour range.

Other possibilities include spraying the material a single colour, whether gold, silver, white or Chinese-lacquer red; substituting red roses or craspedia for the orange helichrysum; or using a limited range of material, such as red-dyed broom bloom, happy flowers and hare's tail grass; and gold-sprayed dyer's greenwood buds.

Ordinary dried-flower gifts, such as the net potpourri bag and the little helichrysum-filled basket, can be dressed up for Christmas. Use small lengths of tinsel or metallic ribbons in Christmas colours; miniature Christmas tree balls are also useful.

Christmas crackers may have had their origins in pagan ritual fires, during which the sound of thunder was simulated; earlier crackers were designed to give out bright flashes of light as well as noise. Contemporary crackers are as harmless as they are pretty. Use scaled-down material of the same flowers and foliage used in a dining-table centrepiece, if there is one, to make the miniature clusters for each cracker. Either glue the sprays directly onto the crackers, or glue each one to a small, oval piece of card and, when dry, glue the card to the cracker. The mini-roses decorating the gold cracker are made of individual dried rose petals, steamed over a kettle until pliable, then curled into a bud shape and wired to a central cluster of broom bloom.

The posy of roses, white delphinium, gold-sprayed honesty pods and silver-sprayed dyer's greenwood suspended on a gold ribbon, could decorate large gift packages; form the centrepiece of an evergreen swag or wreath; or even decorate a gift bottle of wine.

The tiny Christmas wreath is made in the same way as those on page 60, then given several light sprays of silver paint, and, when dry, tied with a red ribbon.

The miniature Christmas tree is built on a preshaped cone of florist's foam, and is a masterpiece of economy. Flower heads and seed pods with broken or very short stems provide the raw material. Some have several coats of gold or silver paint;

Dining Table Arrangement

The dining table is a traditional setting for Christmas flowers and the arrangement shown is equally traditional. The main display, complemented by a pair of matching candle-stick holders, adheres to the general rule that dining table displays should be attractive but not invasive.

Built on a block of florist's foam, the centrepiece started life as an autumnal arrangement, and shows how easily a non-Christmas display can become an archetypically Christmas one. Greeny-brown sprigs of preserved cypress; dried grasses and beech leaves provide mass and general shape: roughly oval with two pointed ends; and gradually changing from flat to mounded towards the centre. Honesty pods and helichrysum add contrasting colour and form.

The transformation involved removing the helichrysums, then giving the remaining arrangement several coats of gold aerosol spray paint. A light, single coat gave the helichrysums a festive air while retaining some of their natural colour. When dry, the helichrysums were returned to the display, together with red rose buds, clusters of nuts, bronze-sprayed pine cones and sprigs of fresh pine and ceanothus.

The two candle-stick holders are small ramekins, each filled with florist's foam packed round a candle. The outside is covered with sphagnum moss held in place with silver reel wire, then sprayed gold. The florist's foam is covered with sprigs of fresh pine and ceanothus; dried roses; and gold-sprayed helichrysum, box and beech leaves.

The wall swag shown – an instant response to the boringly bare wall space behind the table – takes less than five minutes to make, but is nonetheless very effective. Larger branches of pine and ceanothus are wired together with gold-sprayed branches of alder and beech. A red bow hides the wire, and wired, gold-sprayed pine cones add the sparkle.

Evergreen conifer foliage is much slower to wilt, once cut, than deciduous foliage, because the needles are covered in a waxy coating which reduces transpiration. Some broad-leaved evergreens, such as ivy, holly and laurel, are similarly long suffering and both can be combined, as here, with dried material. Such an arrangement will last at least a week, and can quickly be revived by replacing the old evergreen foliage with fresh.

Conifer foliage, evergreens and dried flowers are all very flammable. Although candles look nicer lit, it is safer to substitute an identical pair of candles in plain holders during the time the candles are burning. Flame retardent sprays are available to individuals as well as the trade, from specialist fireproofing firms and some florists. The sprays do not make the material completely fireproof. If candles are lit, they should be non-drip, and never allowed to burn low enough to come in contact with the dried material. Never leave the room when the candles are burning and take care that they do not get knocked over.

The holly, conifers, laurel and other broad-leaved evergreens that are normally used to make Christmas wreaths cannot be faulted. They are richly coloured, traditional, sturdy and reflect perfectly the season they represent. Their one modest drawback is that, being traditional, they are also predictable, perhaps a bit anonymous. Those who feel that a change is as good as a rest, or wish to express personal creativity, might opt for a dried-flower wreath.

A circle of florist's foam forms the foundation, and evenly distributed dried mature hydrangea flower heads, the bulk of the display. Drying hydrangeas is an unpredictable business. The usual method is to dry young flowers at the peak of their colour, in a desiccant; or when older, take the mature heads, which have begun to dry naturally and have a papery feel, and complete the drying process with their resting stems in water. Sometimes, however, hydrangeas dry naturally, while attached to the shrub, and the heads used in this wreath dried this way.

Sprigs of preserved pittosporum, beech and eucalyptus leaves add contrast to the range of pale greens, pinks and mauves of the hydrangeas; and sea lavender adds a lacy delicacy. Echinops thistle heads introduce a circular theme, and silver balls and sequin-waste bows wired to the ring make discreet references to Christmas.

Silver-painted nuts or teasel heads could be substituted for the silver balls, or used in their natural state. Although red and green are the two main colours of Christmas, white just qualifies as a third. A wreath of dried

gypsophila; bleached white hare's tail grass; bleached white quaking grass; honesty seed pods; and dried red rose buds would convey seasonal greetings in a most attractive, if unusual, way.

Almost any wreath of dried material can be converted, with red, white, silver or gold aerosol spray paint, into an instantly identifiable Christmas decoration, although some people consider this approach an insult to the subtle natural colouring of dried material. A combination of pine, larch and cypress cones, together with poppy and echinops seed heads and achillea flower heads, would make a beautifully sculptural sprayed wreath. White spray is particularly attractive, as a fine bone-china like effect results from several light coats.

As house plants, poinsettias make their annual appearance only at Christmas, when their combination of red, petal-like flower bracts and green foliage mirror the traditional colours of this holiday. Pink forms and white forms are also available, and a recent development is a marbled, white and red form.

The poinsettia makes a large shrub or small tree in its native South America and the house plants sold now are a far cry, botanically, from the species originally exhibited by Dr J. R. Poinsett in 1829 at The Pennsylvania Horticultural Society. The poinsettia's potential value as a Christmas decoration was obvious, but its huge size made it impractical, except as a floor-level display. After much experimentation, self-branching cultivars were developed, and chemical dwarfing compounds to keep them small. Poinsettias are induced to flower at Christmas by rigorously controlled growing conditions and limited exposure to light.

A white-flowered poinsettia forms the centre of the display shown; some people prefer the white-flowered form, for its less frenzied colour combination and its rarity value. The arrangement of dried white flowers and pine cones would be equally suitable for a red poinsettia, especially as there is no dried green foliage or red dried flower that can hold its own against a red poinsettia or its green leaves, except perhaps fiercely dyed material. The red of a poinsettia and the orange-brown of a plastic flower pot are a particularly unfortunate combination, and this setting of

white flowers would be a vast improvement.

A wire mesh ring filled with dried florist's foam built round the flower pot forms the foundation, although a suitably-sized ring of florist's foam could also be used. White xeranthemum flowers and buds, enlivened with sprigs of dill and statice and wired-up pine cones, are inserted into the foundation, until

both it and the flower pot are fully concealed, and reindeer moss is tucked round the base as necessary.

Poinsettias have a habit of dropping their lower leaves with age, and more dried flowers could be gradually added, to conceal the bare lower stems. When the poinsettia has finished its useful display life, another house plant could be substituted.

Church Flowers

Bold arrangements that can be seen from a distance are most effective, as is a single colour scheme for the pedestal, pew end and individual table arrangements. The colours should stand out well against the background, whether wood, stone or plain painted wall. This is a particularly important consideration with dried flowers, as many of them are neutral in colour. If decorating a church for a wedding, the flowers should ideally follow the same colour scheme as those carried by the bridal party.

Visit the church beforehand to take measurements and discuss any special requirements with the staff. Pedestals and containers are usually available from the church. Check whether pew end arrangements can be attached by ribbon-covered wires hooked over the pew ends, or for pew ends with horizontal indentations, ribbons can be slotted through and then tied at the back. Every pew end can be decorated; a pair in front, middle and back; or just the front few pews. Although aisles vary in width, dried material is very vulnerable to breakage, and pew end arrangements should not protrude more than 20cm (8in).

Because dried flowers and foliage tend to shed bits and pieces, especially in the course of being arranged, try to prepare as many of the smaller arrangements as possible at home. This also removes much of the tension, provided that you have adequate storage and transport facilities.

Although churches vary in size and layout, the steps leading to the chancel and altar rail are traditional positions for large-scale arrangements, particularly for weddings. Swags or floral ropes attached to pillars are another possibility, but again, check with those in authority before beginning your arrangements. There are often strict regulations about the floral decorations of the altar, although with dried material there is no risk of water spillage! Lastly, sort out what is going to happen to the arrangements – whether they are to be removed immediately after the event or some time later – and arrange for the church to be left spotless and free of all dried flower remains.

This rich red and gold arrangement is autumnal in feeling, and is made up of lady's mantle, dyer's greenwood, morrison, dyed phalaris grass and roses. The foundation is a rectangular block of florist's foam, with red ribbon wired through the top. The florist's foam is then hung vertically from the ribbon, and the flowers, starting with an even layer of lady's mantle, are positioned on it, working from the outside inwards.

Small clusters of dried grass are used to establish a rough symmetry, and are followed by the intensely gold morrison and the rounded heads of dyer's greenwood, so that the sides and front of the florist's foam are evenly covered. The roses, on natural stems, are added last. Rose clusters are wired together before insertion, with a large cluster forming the focal point. The ribbon bow is wired into the bottom when the arrangement is complete.

An alternative choice of flowers, to create a spring or summery feel, is gypsophila, cream broom bloom, pink roses and love-in-a-mist seed pods.

The flowers for this formal triangular arrangement are the same as those used in the pew end display. It is not as solid because there is less florist's foam to hide and more space to fill.

The three points of the triangle and outline are established first, with the traditional proportion of the height of the flowers equalling at least twice the height of the container. The shape is then infilled with phalaris, dyer's greenwood, lady's mantle, and morrison. The phalaris heads are used singly, and because their stems are thin, are inserted first, before the florist's foam becomes crowded. The roses, again left on natural stems and wired into clusters of three to five, are positioned last.

Front-facing arrangements are liable to topple forwards, so angle some of the material slightly backwards for balance; work it round the sides, for visual and structural reasons; and ensure that the container is adequately weighted. Arrangements such as this are easier done *in situ,* as transportation can be a problem.

Wedding Flowers

The idea of doing an entire wedding in dried flowers is unusual, but not outrageously so. More and more brides are choosing silk or polyester flowers for their weddings, because the bouquets can be kept indefinitely afterwards as mementoes and family heirlooms. Bouquets of fresh flowers sometimes can be dried after the event, but this is a time-consuming and expensive exercise. Individual flowers have to be unwired, sometimes taken apart petal by petal, then put back together again and re-wired after being dried or otherwise preserved. Then, too, the process has to be started while the flowers are still fresh, which may mean before the wedding festivities are over.

For brides with one eye on posterity, and a commitment to the natural as opposed to the artificial, dried flowers offer a good compromise. Additionally, dried flower bouquets, posies, circlets, corsages and baskets can be made well in advance, without the often tense race against time that dealing with fresh flowers entails.

The wedding flowers that follow illustrate two possible themes: a winter wedding, based on white, cream and green; and a spring or summer wedding, based on pale pink. Obviously, styles and colours suggested can be altered or substituted, according to personal taste and skill.

If there are to be bridesmaids and flower girls, then it is only courteous for the bride to consult them about the choice of floral material and colour, and the style of their bouquets and floral headdresses. On the other hand, committee decisions, based on compromise, are not always the best ones, especially where taste or design is concerned. The bride should retain, and exercise, if necessary, the right to make the final choices.

The old-fashioned tradition of the bride throwing her bouquet to a bevy of waiting bridesmaids doesn't really work with dried flowers, especially if the bride wants to preserve the bouquet as an heirloom. In this case, arrange to have a small posy of fresh flowers, perhaps even an informal bunch of garden flowers, to continue in the spirit of the tradition.

This wedding bouquet is elegant and unusual, but its main virtue is how quick and easy it is to make. No wiring is required, so the bouquet would be a sensible choice for a beginner or if time is short.

The bouquet is built up on a commercially available bouquet handle, which is plastic and topped with a small perforated container holding florist's foam. The foam sold with it is that used for fresh flowers; remove and replace it with florist's foam for dried flowers. Alternatively, glue a small block of florist's foam, about 12.5cm (5in) across, onto the wooden handle of a skipping rope, and doubly secure the foam to the handle with medium-thick reel wire, or wire mesh stapled to the handle.

Rest the handle in a weighted empty bottle. Starting with shortish stems of dried white achillea and dill, begin at the centre. Working outwards, build up an oval shape, slightly broader at the top than the bottom, introducing delphinium, barley and unripe buds of dyer's greenwood. The bouquet should be densest in the centre, gradually becoming more open and airy towards the edges. Use longer stems working away from the centre, saving the longest for the bottom of the bouquet, to give a tiny hint of a trail.

Although there is no strict symmetry, space the barley relatively evenly apart, especially round the edge, where it stands out in silhouette. Add the cluster of dyer's greenwood towards the end, followed by the wired ribbon. Conceal the handle with ribbon trails. Pink or yellow dried roses could be added for colour.

This pretty posy for a bridesmaid or flower girl follows a traditional pattern of concentric rings of flowers built up round a single central flower or bud. Unlike the matching unwired bride's bouquet, the Victorian posy is made of small bunches of flowers wired together, then taped to support wires which form the handle. Although smaller than the bride's bouquet, this posy takes more time and effort to make, and relatively more material for its size.

Using silver wire, wire up small bunches of white dill, statice, delphinium florets and achillea. Tape the bunches to 0.71mm support wires. Because the support wires are ultimately hidden, use only as much tape as is necessary to firmly attach the bunches to their supports. Individually wire up and tape the dyer's greenwood buds. Holding the central bud, build up a tight circle of white flowers around and slightly lower than the bud, then tape. Trim the support wires for the handle gradually, so that the handle is not thick and unsightly. Continue with the next circle, alternating bunches of flowers with evenly spaced dyer's greenwood buds. Each concentric circle should be slightly lower than the one made previously, to give a mounded effect. Each successive circle of wires is bent at a sharper angle where they meet the central handle. This gradually increases in thickness, as more and more wires are added.

The posy shown is 20cm (8in) in diameter, excluding the lace edging, and has four concentric circles; more or less may be needed, according to the material and desired diameter.

Once all the floral material is in position, wind silver reel wire or tape round the support wires, to secure them. Trim the wires to the desired thickness, then cut them to form a handle approximately 15cm (6in) long. Cover with several layers of tape. Slip the handle through a stiffened lacy circlet, pushed up as far as it will go, secure with wire, then tape. Wire a single head of barley underneath the circlet. Cover the handle with a ribbon, then finish

with a wired ribbon bow, repeating the theme of the bride's bouquet.

Lace circlets are commercially available but a traditional alternative is an edging of foliage, such as fronds of preserved fern, beech or eucalyptus. Making each ring a different colour, or using alternating colours, would emphasize the roundness.

The buttonhole is simply two buds of dyer's greenwood and a single ear of barley wired together, then taped.

The dried flowers in this swag are attached to a foundation of fresh Mexican orange. Its shiny evergreen foliage provides bulk and effective contrast for the white delphinium, dill and statice. Combining dried flowers and fresh foliage in this way is also economical, in time as well as money. Encircling the table top with a single thick swag, rather than draping loops around the sides, is another economy, but the end result is still one of opulence.

Measure the table, allowing for loops, if wished; a long piece of string to roughly indicate the size and spacing of loops is useful. Allow for a generous overlap where the two ends meet. Remove 10-15cm (4-6in) sprigs of foliage from the branches of the Mexican orange; a few tiny sprigs of white-variegated ivy are also used, as optional extras. Although using longer sprigs, or whole stems, might seem tempting, they are less flexible and can give an awkwardly angular and sparse effect, especially if the swag is looped. Using medium-weight reel wire, begin making a dense rope by wiring together overlapping sprigs. Gradually thicken the density of foliage towards the half-way mark, for the front of the table, and reduce the density in equal proportion as you proceed towards the other end. Before adding dried material, check the length around the table and make any adjustments necessary.

Using silver reel wire, wire up small bunches of white delphinium, statice and white dill. Lay the foliage rope out flat, then line up the little bunches, interspersed with ears of barley and thick buds of dyer's

greenwood, evenly along one side, to get a rough idea of the distribution. Allow for a concentration of dried material in the centre, where the foliage is thickest, and keep some in reserve, for last-minute corrections.

Using medium-weight reel wire, attach the flower bunches, barley and dyer's greenwood, to the floral rope, starting at one end and working towards the other. When finished, and with a helper if possible, fix the swag to the tablecloth, using long dressmaker's pins. Because the swag is made in one position and moved to another, final adjustments will be necessary: changing the direction of a few barley heads; concealing wires that were previously hidden; repositioning material that sticks out dangerously; or infilling holes. Allow plenty of time.

The proportions of fresh foliage to dried flowers are roughly equal in this swag, but a dried flower swag could be enlivened with a few small sprigs of fresh foliage; a swag of fresh foliage could have small posies of dried flowers attached at regular intervals; or, like a drop necklace, a single large dried flower arrangement could form the centre of a fresh foliage swag. Raffia swags braided with ribbons would be particularly suitable for looping around a table, with little dried flower clusters attached to each point.

The tiny silver cake-top vase holds a miniature posy, inserted in florists' foam and encircled with fresh leaves. The knife spray consists of a single leaf and tiny bunch of flowers, wired together, then tied to the knife with

thin ribbon, which also conceals the wires.

Another way of decorating a cake with dried flowers is to make a miniature version of either the brides' bouquet or the bridesmaid's posies, then to either place it directly on the cake, or to insert a posy pick in the cake to hold it. Posy picks are available from cake decorating shops and some florists. If using this method, the pick will need to be supplied to the baker when the cake is ordered.

Pink delphinium, pink achillea and palest pink gypsophila could be used instead of white flowers. Other tough, broad-leaved evergreens include smilax, laurel, rhododendron, butcher's broom, elaeagnus and ivy, both in their green and many variegated forms, ivy's woody, flowering growth sometimes called tree ivy, would make an exquisite swag, especially with its clusters of green, unripe berries. Florist's cypress is easily available and inexpensive, but can look mournful. The autumnal church flowers shown on page 106 would make an impressive swag with glycerined beech foliage as the foundation.

Unless you are very experienced at wiring flowers, allow two days for making this curved shower bride's bouquet. A work surface that can be left undisturbed is useful, as are large empty jars in which to store the partially made components. Two large florist's bunches of dried roses and cream broom bloom are used to make this bouquet; three large bunches each of delphinium, rhodanthe and oat grass; and one bunch of pink agrostis.

Using silver reel wire, start by wiring tiny individual bunches, no more than 3cm (1½in) long, each containing one type of flower. Use three or four delphinium florets or agrostis sprigs; and two or three sprigs of cream broom bloom, rhodanthe or oat grass per bunch. Wire the rose buds singly, then into seven bunches of three and one bunch of five, as required.

Wire up all the flowers and seed heads; any extras can be used to make little corsages, buttonholes or name-card or place setting decorations. As you finish wiring each bunch, tape approximately a third of the wire with cream or green tape, then put the bunches into jars, separated according to kind.

The next stage is to construct the eight sections which make up the bouquet. The 30cm (12in) bottom section is made first. It is the largest, longer and thicker than others, roughly triangular in shape. It is built up on a 0.71 or 0.90 support wire, which is manipulated into a slight curve inwards and to one side. Using half-width tape, add small bunches to the support wire from the bottom upwards. Gradually thicken the section as you work upwards, by incorporating more little bunches, each tightly overlapping the next; and by taping them to additional 0.71 support wires which are then taped, at a slight angle, to the central one, rather like the branches of a fishbone cotoneaster. One third of the way up, wire in a single rose, and, very near the top, a cluster of three roses. End with approximately 30cm (12in) of taped support wire; no other wire should be visible.

Build the uppermost, top section, next, in the same way. Curve the support wire in the opposite direction, and make the section roughly half the size of the bottom one, about 15cm (6in) long, again beginning with a 30cm (12in) support wire. Make the central posy next, around five rose buds wired into a tight bunch.

Using tape or silver reel wire, tape or wire the three main sections together, into a continuous, subtle curve, which returns slightly inwards at the top and bottom. Bend the top and bottom support wires parallel to the central support wire, which should be in line with the central group of roses, providing a handle directly behind the focal point. This gives the final overall length, the basic shield shape, and the beginning of a handle.

Make the five intermediate, wedge-shaped sections, as shown, each including a cluster of roses towards the top, and each taped on a 0.71 support wire. To emphasize the curved shape, make the bunches on the outside of the curve longer and larger than those on the inside of the curve, though still with the same number of roses. Wire the intermediate bunches tightly into the main framework, using silver reel wire or tape, and bend the support wires to match the angle of the handle. Be careful that the bending point remains in the same place and does not travel downwards. Continue the shield shape by curving the support wires slightly backwards from the centre, like inward curving spokes of a wheel.

Look at the overall effect, and where there are small gaps, use infill bunches, made of single sprigs, or two or three sprigs, attached to support wires. Eight infill bunches are used in this bouquet, but the number necessary can vary.

When the infill bunches are in position and you are satisfied that the bouquet is evenly dense, cut the handle to a length of 15cm (6in). Using silver reel wire or tape, wire or tape round the support wires, then tape over the wires to secure them. Cover the handle with ribbon, either glued or pinned to the top. Add ribbon bows and trails if wished, attaching them at the top of the handle.

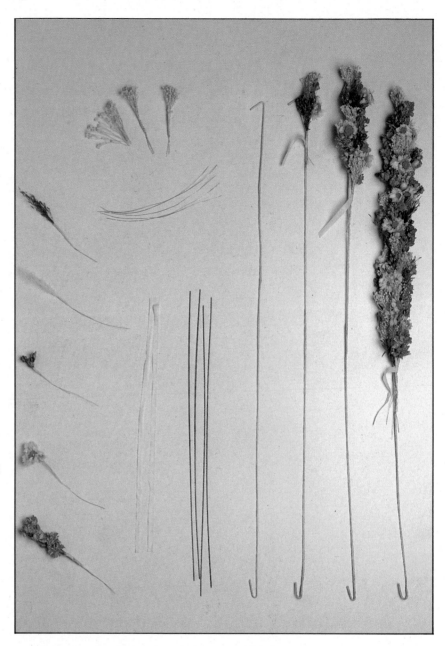

Form the basic shape from two pairs of overlapping 0.71 wires, then cover with tape, to give a 60cm (24in) length of straight wire. A circlet for an adult or adolescent should have an approximately 57.5cm (23in) circumference; the extra 2.5cm (1in) allows for a small hook at each end.

Bend over the end 15mm (½in) to create small hooks, and leave the rest of the wire straight. Using silver wire, wire up small bunches of flowers, such as the roses, delphiniums, gypsophila, agrostis and oat grass, each type in separate bunches. Bind each bunch with tape, leaving approximately 2.5cm (1in) of stem. Begin taping the bunches to the top end of the straight wire, leaving a slight gap to allow for hooking. Using half-width tape and working with the wire flat, gradually build up the bunches in overlapping layers. Keep the bunches tightly packed and even, so that no wire shows, and take the flowers three-quarters of the way around the wire. The bit of taped wire that isn't covered with flowers will form the inside of the circlet, where it rests on the head.

When all the flowers are attached, form an even circle, bending the wire round a little at a time, then hook the two ends together. Conceal the hook with a toning or matching 15mm (½in) ribbon bow, made by pinching together two, four or six loops, then securing the loops with silver wire and attaching the wire to the circlet. Any minor adjustments in fitting can be made by removing a bunch of flowers from either side of the hooks, or by enlarging the hook, to take in any slack. Keep until needed resting on tissue paper in a covered box in a dry place.

There are several variations. You can add extra bows, evenly spaced out, around the circlet; add them as you tape on the flowers, not afterwards. Trailing ribbons can be added; the same length as the ribbon at the back, or shorter. Beads, pearls or feathers can be inserted, wiring and taping them as for flowers. The flowers can also be built up and taped from each end so they point towards the middle.

Floral Comb

Wire up very small bunches, as above, and wire up each rose separately. Using silver reel wire about 45cm (18in) long, begin wrapping wire around the top of the comb, going between the teeth and inserting the ends of the flowers as you wrap. Finish by threading the silver wire through the wire web at the back. Don't worry about the appearance of the back of the comb, as it will not be visible.

The headdress is made in the same way as that for the bride (page 114), omitting the roses and oat grass.

Fill the basket with crumpled 2.5cm (1in) wire mesh, then attach the wire mesh securely to the sides of the basket. Push 4-6 short lengths of silver reel wire through the basket, from the inside out. Loop the silver reel wire back into the basket and over the wire mesh, then twist the silver wire two or three times.

To decorate the handle, stick one end of 15mm (½in) ribbon down with mastic, then wind it round, overlapping. Cut off any excess ribbon and attach the end with mastic. Insert a bow on one or both sides, if wished, at this stage.

Remembering to leave enough space between tallest flower and handle, begin filling the basket. The delphinium, agrostis, roses and oat grass in this basket did not need

wiring, although the gypsophila, used for infill once the general mass is established, is wired with 0.71 wire.

For extra fragrance, fill the basket with potpourri, packed in solidly. Wire all of the bunches of flowers and use the potpourri to secure the flowers into the desired position.

You could make a garland of flowers for the basket, similar to the headdress, then arrange the flowers inside.

For a flower ball, or pompom, buy a pre-shaped ball of florist's foam or polystyrene. Wire both ends of a 15mm (½in) ribbon, about 45cm (18in) long, to a 0.71 wire, and fold the ribbon in half. Push the wire straight through the middle of the foam until it comes out at the bottom. Make a small hook at the bottom of the wire, then hook it into the ball by pulling upwards. Hang the ribbon loop over the end of a towel rail or the back of a chair. Wire the flowers into compact bunches, first wiring up stemless florets, such as delphinium, if necessary, using silver wire; no taping is necessary. Cut the silver wire and stems so that a 15mm (½in) stub remains. Start at the top of the ball and insert the stems evenly and densely into the florist's foam, working gradually towards the bottom.

Rest the finished ball on tissue paper in a covered box, together with a few extra made-up bunches. Before use, gently tease out any of the flowers on the bottom that may have become compacted, or replace them with the spare bunches.

As a variation, add a bow to the bottom of the ball, using the same ribbon as the loop. Hook the bow through the wire before inserting the flowers.

After the wedding, you can convert the ball into a floral tree, first removing the ribbons and a few bunches of flowers from the base (see page 88).

Corsage
Using silver wire, wire up the bunches, as above, then tape with half-width tape. Starting with one bunch, tape bunch after bunch onto it, into the desired shape, adding a focal point if wished. The flowers should wrap three-quarters of the way round the corsage, leaving a flat back. You should end up with a thick stem, about 6.5cm (2½in) long. Cut the stem, if necessary, then finish with a florist's pin.

Net Bag with Almonds
Using silver wire, wire up a small bunch of flowers and seed heads, as above, but using a mixture of flowers instead of single types. Tape with half-width tape. Cut 15cm (6in) circles out of net; you can use a side plate as a template. Push a pencil into the middle of each circle, to form a narrow tube shape, then carefully dip the cut edge into a fabric dye, to make a 6mm (¼in) tinted border. Spread out to dry on tissue paper.

When dry, fill with two or three almonds, then use narrow toning ribbon to tie the bag shut and to attach the floral sprig.

Dried Plant Material

T he range and variety of plant material available is vast, and it would be impossible to show an example of every single dried flower, leaf and seed head. The photographs on the following pages show some of the popular kinds of dried plant material. All the material illustrated has been either grown or gathered from the wild, then dried by the methods described in the section on 'Preserving Flowers and Foliage'. These plants were used in the arrangements in this book, combined with commercially produced dried material, both dyed and natural, as well as non-floral material such as pine cones, fantasy flowers and ribbons.

Because common names can differ from country to country, and even from region to region within a country, the plants are listed alphabetically by Latin names, with common names in brackets. The charts which begin on page 140 are also listed by Latin names, and include such important information as harvesting techniques and suitable methods of drying for each plant.

Acanthus spp   Acanthus

Achillea spp   Achillea

Achillea millefolium Yarrow or milfoil

Aegopodium podagravia Ground elder

Alchemilla mollis Lady's mantle

Allium schoenoprasum Chive

Alopecurus pratensis　　　　　　　　Meadow foxtail

Alstroemeria spp　　　　　　　　Alstroemeria

Althaea rosea　　　　　　　Hollyhock

Ammobium alatum　　　　　Winged everlasting daisy

Aquilegia × hybrida   Columbine

Arctium lappa   Burdock

Artemisia vulgaris   Mugwort

Astilbe arendsii   False goat's beard

Avena sativa   Oats (field)

Barbarea spp   Sweet rocket

Brassica napus   Rape (field)

Calendula officinalis   Pot marigold

Campanula carpatica, persicifolia   Bellflower

Centaurea cyanus   Cornflower

Centaurea spp   Knapweed/hardhead

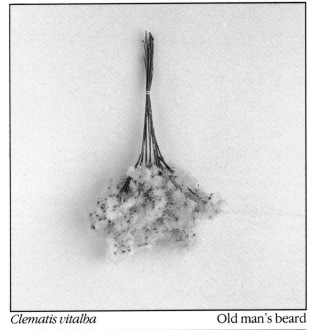

Clematis vitalba   Old man's beard

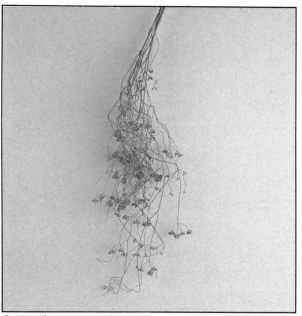

Coriandrum sativum Coriander

Crocosmia, masonorum Montbretia

Dactyluis glomerate Cocksfoot grass

Delphinium spp Larkspur

Dianthus barbatus   Sweet William

Digitalis purpurea   Foxglove

Dipsacus spp   Teasel

Doronicum cordatum   Leopard's bane

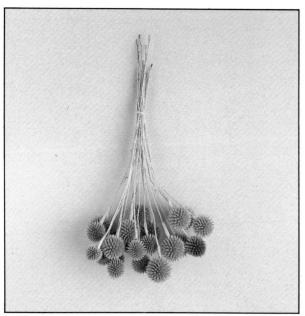

Echinops ritro   Echinops

Eleagnus spp   Eleagnus

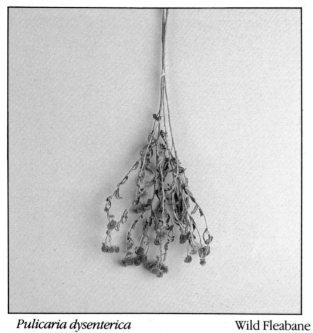

Pulicaria dysenterica   Wild Fleabane

Epilobium angustifolium   Rosebay willowherb

Erica, spp *calluna vulgaris*   Heather (wild, garden)

Eucalyptus spp   Eucalyptus/gum tree

Fagus sylvatica   Beech (copper/green)

Galeopsis tetrahit   Common hempnettle

Geranium ibericum   Crane's bill

Hedera spp   Ivy

Helichrysum bracteatum   Straw flower

Helipterum, manglesii   Helipterum daisy

Helleborus spp   Hellebore

Heracleum sphondylium   Hogweed, cow parsnip

Holcus lanatus   Yorkshire fog

Hordeum vulgare   Barley (field)

Humulus lupulus　　　　　　　　　　　　Hop

Hypericum calycinum　　　　　　　St John's wort

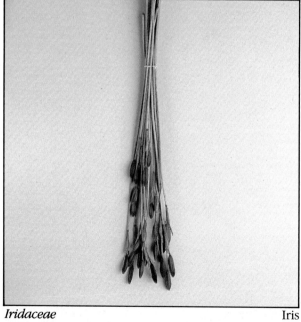

Iridaceae　　　　　　　　　　　　　　Iris

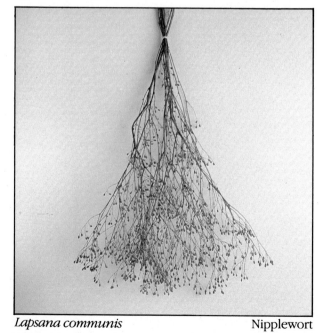

Lapsana communis　　　　　　　　　Nipplewort

Lavandula angus tifolia   Lavender

Leucanthemum vulgare   Oxeye daisy

Limonium sinuatum   Statice

Linum usitatissimum   Common flax

Lunaria   Honesty

Lychnis spp   Rose campion

Lysimachia punctata   Yellow loosestrife

Matricaria recutita   Mayweed

Mentha spp   Garden mint

Muscari spp   Grape hyacinth

Nigella damascena   Love-in-a-mist

Oenothera spp   Evening primrose

Origanum vulgare   Marjoram (wild)

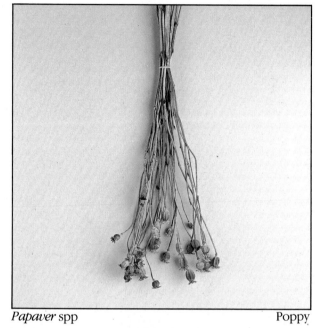

Papaver spp   Poppy

Petroselinum crispum   Parsley

Phalaris arundinacea   Canary grass

Phleum pratense   Cat's tail/timothy

Phragmites communis   Great reed

Cupressus Family   Conifer

Plantago lanceolata   Ribwort

Plantago media   Hoary plantain

Polygonum bistorta   Bistort

Polygonum persicaria   Redshank,

Prunus laurocerasus   Laurel

Rudbeckia spp   Rudbeckia (annual)

Rudbeckia laciniata   Rudbeckia

Santolina chamaecyparissus   Lavender cotton

Scabiosa hybrid   Paper moon scabious

Sedum spp   Stonecrop

Silene dioica   Campion (red/white)

Sisyrinchium striatum   Satin flower

Solidago canadensis   Golden rod

Triticum aestirum   Wheat (field)

Briza, Lagurus, and other ornamental grasses   Ferns

Veronica longifolia/spicata   Speedwell

Xeranthemum abbum   Everlasting Flower

PLANT LATIN NAME	COMMON NAME	MATERIAL TYPE S=Seed head F=Flower L=Leaf B=Branch Material Type	RECOMMENDED TREATMENT PROCESS A=Air dry G=Glycerine T=Antifreeze P=Pressing Treatment Process	Special notes on harvesting
Acanthus spp	Acanthus	S	A	After flowering of top buds, when stem tip starts to harden
Acer saccharinum	Silver maple	L	A, G	Just before full autumn colouring, as leaves start to fall naturally, dry flat
Achillea spp	Achillea	F	A	Best bloom, before head fully open and colour fades
Achillea millefolium	Yarrow or milfoil	F	A	Prime bloom, before whiteness fades
Acroclinium	Australian everlasting	F	A	Mid to full bloom, before all yellow centre stamens visible
Aegopodium podagravia	Ground elder	S	A	At full green seed head
Agrostis spp	Bent grass	F, S	A	Mature stem
Agrostemma githago	Corn cockle	S	A	After purple flower, seed head stage
Alchemilla mollis	Lady's mantle	F	A	Mid to full bloom before yellow fades
Allium schoenoprasum	Chive	F	A	Just at full purple bloom
Allium spp	Ornamental onion	F, S	A	Prime bloom petals all round the 'ball', or after petal fall at green send stage
Allium spp	Leek	F, S	A	Prime bloom petals all round the 'ball', or after petal fall at green seed stage
Alopecurus pratensis	Meadow foxtail	F, S	A	In flower or after, at brightest green colour of stems
Althaea rosea	Hollyhock	F, S	A	Top stem flowers in bloom, fully formed green seed pods at bottom of stem
Alstroemeria spp	Alstroemeria	S	A	After petal fall, when green seed pods just coming to maturity (do not leave too late)
Ammobium alatum	Winged everlasting daisy	F	A	Two-thirds bloom open
Anemone hupehensis	Japanese anemone	S	A	After petal fall
Anthemis cupaniana	Chamomile shrub	F, L	A, G	Full leaf, and at fading flower, pluck out petals
Antirrhinum spp	Snapdragon	S	A	Seed pod stage, green stems turning to brown
Aquilegia × hybrida	Columbine	S	A	After flowering, mature green seed pods
Arctium lappa	Burdock	S	A	After flowering, and plant is fully mature at growing tips
Artemisia vulgaris	Mugwort	F, S	A	Mature plant at growing tips, still silver grey/green
Aruncus diolcus	Goat's beard	F, S	A	Immediately after flowering
Astilbe arendsii	False goat's beard	F, S	A	After flowering
Avena sativa	Oats (field)	S	A	Green fully formed ears, as green/yellow, and golden before corns drop
Barbarea spp	Sweet Rocket	S, A	A	After petal fall, before seed pods split
Betula pendula	Silver birch	S, B	G	Catkin stage with leaves, or mature leaves only
Borago officinalis	Borage	S, F	A	At flowering, and past flowering
Brassica napus	Rape (field)	S	A	Green seed pod stage, or later green going brown, as seeds shatter
Briza media	Pearl/quaking grass	F, S	A	After flowering, as pearls fully develop, well before natural die back
Buddleia spp	Buddleia	S	A	At flowering, and as ripe brown, before seed pods split
Buxus sempervirens	Box	L, B	T	Mature leaves
Calendula officinalis	Pot marigold	S, F	A	Green mature seed formation, flower prime bloom
Campanula carpatica, persicifolia	Bellflower	S	A	After flowering, as pods turn green/buff, before seed pots open, or after opening
Carpinus betulus	Hornbeam keys	S	A	Mature, before natural shedding from tree
Catananche caerulea	Cupid's dart	F	A	Mid bloom
Centaurea cyanus	Cornflower	S, F	A	Flower half open up to prime, or after petal fall for seed head only
Centaurea spp	Knapweed/hardhead	F, S	A	In mid flower, or pods dark nut brown
Chrysanthemum parthenium	Feverfew	F, S	A	Mid bloom, or late bloom and pluck out petals

PLANT LATIN NAME	COMMON NAME	MATERIAL TYPE S=Seed head F=Flower L=Leaf B=Branch	RECOMMENDED TREATMENT PROCESS A=Air dry G=Glycerine T=Antifreeze P=Pressing	
		Material Type	Treatment Process	Special notes on harvesting
Clarkia elegans	Clarkia	F, S	A	After flowering, when seed pods full but still green or later when dried brown and seeds shatter
Clematis spp	Clematis	S	A	Pick at whirl stage, before fluffs form
Clematis vitalba	Old man's beard	S	A	Pick when whirls formed, but not in fluff
Coriandrum sativum	Coriander	S	A	Seed pod stage
Cortaderia selloana	Pampas	F, S	A	As plumes protrude from stem tops, and before becoming fluffy
Crocosmia, masonorum	Montbretia	S, L	A	Seed pods going orange/brown; leaf mature
Cupressus spp	Cypress		A, T	Mature green fronds, or mature variegated fronds
Dactylis glomerata	Cocksfoot grass	F, S	A	After flowering, brightest green colour of heads
Daucus carota	Carrot (wild)	S	A	Naturally dried off, deep brown seed heads and stems
Delphinium hybrids spp	Delphinium	S	A	After petal fall, before seed turn dark brown and split
Delphinium spp	Larkspur	S	A	After petal fall, before seed turn dark brown and split
Dianthus barbatus	Sweet William	F	A	Head two-thirds open bloom
Digitalis purpurea	Foxglove	S	A	After flowering, green maturing brown stems, before seed shatter
Dipsacus spp	Teasel	S	A	Green turning brown, late after frost dark brown as seeds disperse
Doronicum cordatum	Leopard's bane	S	A	Pluck out petals for green seed back; hang dry upsidedown
Echinops ritro	Echinops	S	A	Just after blue flowering, as thistle ball spikes become mature
Eleagnus spp	Eleagnus	L	A, T	Mature leaf at growing tips
Erigeron spp	Garden Fleabane	F, S	A	In flower
Endymion non-scriptus	Bluebell	S	A	Crisp brown seeds and stems, at seed dispersement
Epilobium angustifolium	Rosebay willowherb	F, S	A	Quick dry in purple full bloom, or cut at green seed stage, before fluffing occurs
Erica, spp *calluna vulgaris*	Heather (wild, garden)	F	A, G, T	Just before full bloom
Eryngium spp	Sea holly	F, S	A	Mature stems, mid to full bloom, and when dried off naturally
Eschscholzia californica	Eschscholzia	S	A	Green fully formed seed stage
Eucalyptus spp	Eucalyptus/gum tree	L	G	Mature leaf up majority of stem
Euonymus europaeus	Spindle berry	S	A	Mature pink seed pods, do not leave too late
Fagus sylvatica	Beech (copper/green)	L, B	G	Mature leaves
Fagus sylvatica	Beech nuts	S	A	Mature, before natural splitting and seed shatter
Foeniculum vulgare	Fennel	F, S	A	Green seed stage
Fraximus excelsior	Ash keys	S	A	Mature, as natural shedding from tree starts
Galeopsis tetrahit	Common hempnettle	S	A	After flowering, fully mature and natural leaf drop stage
Geranium ibericum	Crane's bill	S, F	A	After petal fall, stems turning green/brown
Godetia grandiflora	Godetia	F, S	A	After flowering, when seed pods full but still green or later when dried brown and seeds shatter
Hedera spp	Ivy	L	A, T	Mature leaf
Helichrysum bracteatum	Straw flower	F	A	Full bloom, before yellow centre stamens too visible
Helipterum, manglesii	Helipterum daisy	F	A	In mid to full bloom, before all yellow centre too visible
Helleborus spp	Hellebore	F, L	T	Full green flower, or mature leaf
Heracleum sphondylium	Hogweed, cow parsnip	S	A	Mature, green/brown, before seeds disperse; later at brown dead stage

PLANT LATIN NAME	COMMON NAME	MATERIAL TYPE S=Seed head F=Flower L=Leaf B=Branch	RECOMMENDED TREATMENT PROCESS A=Air dry G=Glycerine T=Antifreeze P=Pressing	
		Material Type	Treatment Process	Special notes on harvesting
Holcus lanatus	Yorkshire fog	F, S	A	Pink flowering stage for colour, or buff colour naturally dried off
Hordeum vulgare	Barley (field)	S	A	Green fully formed ears, as green/yellow, but before heads turn over
Humulus lupulus	Hop	F	A	Flowers pale green in mid to full bloom, only small buds remain on stem tops
Hydrangea spp	Hydrangea	F	A	Cut as petals start to feel papery
Hypericum calycinum	St Johns wort	S	A	Black seed stage, brown mature leaf
Iberis saxatilis	Candytuft	S	A	When naturally dried off, at seed shatter
Ipomea hybrids	Morning glory	S	A	Seed pod stage, green going brown
Iridaceae	Iris	S	A	Ripe seed pod, before seed shatter
Lagurus ovatus	Hare's tail	F, S	A	After flowering, as green tails, or silver/green tails when more mature
Lapsana communis	Nipplewort	S	A	Mature, going brown, at seed shatter stage
Lavandula angustifolia	Lavender	F	A	Mid to prime bloom
Leucanthemum vulgare	Oxeye daisy	F, S	A	Mid to full bloom before white petals discolour, or pluck out for seed back only
Ligustrum ovalifolium	Privet	L, B	T	Mature leaves
Limonium sinuatum	Statice	F	A	Mid to best bloom, before head fully open
Linum usitatissimum	Common flax	F, S	A	Past flowering, when yellow seed case becomes fully visible
Lunaria	Honesty	S	A	Green seed pods stage, or fully mature, when seed case opens, silver centre exposed
Lychnis dioica	Campion	S	A	Pods mature, green, going brown, before seed shatter
Lychnis spp	Rose campion	S	A	After flowering, and starting to dry naturally. For silver colouring do not leave too long
Lysimachia punctata	Yellow loosestrife	F, S	A	After flowering
Lythrum salicaria	Purple loosestrife	S	A	After petal fall, with good autumn brown colour of stem
Mahonia spp	Mahonia	L	A, T	Mature leaf, or in autumn colours
Matricaria recutita	Mayweed	S, F	A	Prime bloom
Mentha spp	Garden mint	F	A	Two-thirds stem in prime bloom
Moluccella laevis	Bells of Ireland	F	G	Just maturing, green
Muscari spp	Grape hyacinth	S	A	Crisp buff colour and seeds shed
Nigella damascena	Love-in-a-mist	F, S	A	At full bloom, mature green seed pod stage, before splitting, or brown ripe as seeds shatter
Oenothera spp	Evening primrose	S	A	Mature green tip of stems, or going brown and seed pods opening
Origanum vulgare	Marjoram (wild)	S	A	Mid pink bloom for three-quarters of stem, do not leave too late, as flowers become fluff
Papaver spp	Poppy	S	A	Fully formed green seed pod, before splitting
Pastinaca sativa	Parsnip (wild)	S	A	After flowering, before browning and seeds shed from stems
Petroselinum crispum	Parsley	L, F	A	Prime bloom, and mature green leaf
Phalaris arundinacea	Canary grass	F, S	A	After flowering, as tops are good green, before turning to beige
Phleum pratense	Cat's tail/timothy	F, S	A	In flower or after, at brightest green colour of stems
Physalis alkekenji	Chinese lantern	F	A	Orange pod stage, do not leave too late for good colours
Phragmites communis	Great reed	F, S	A	In flower
Plantago lanceolata	Ribwort	S	A	After flowering, at green seed stage
Plantago media	Hoary plantain	S	A	After flowering, at green seed stage
Polygonatum multiflorum	Solomon's seal	F, S	G	Mature stem
Polygonum bistorta	Bistort	F	A	Full pink bloom

PLANT LATIN NAME	COMMON NAME	MATERIAL TYPE S=Seed head F=Flower L=Leaf B=Branch Material Type	RECOMMENDED TREATMENT PROCESS A=Air dry G=Glycerine T=Antifreeze P=Pressing Treatment Process	Special notes on harvesting
Polygonum persicaria	Redshank, willow weed	F, S	A	Prime flower, and well before seed shatter
Prunus laurocerasus	Laurel	L, B	T	Mature leaves
Pyrethrum spp	Pyrethrum	S	A	After flowering, or pluck out faded petals
Rheum rhaponticum	Rhubarb	F, S	A	At full flower, or immediately after
Rosmarinus officinalis	Rosemary	L, F	A, T	Mature leaf, or early flowering
Rudbeckia spp	Rudbeckia (annual)	S	A	At full/past bloom, pluck out petals, retain brown centre knob only
Rudbeckia laciniata	Rudbeckia (perennial)	S	A	After petal fall, seed head hard dark green/brown
Rumex spp	Sorrel	F, S	A, G, T	At flowering, and good colour red/brown seed stage, well before natural seed shatter
Rumex crispus	Curled dock	F, S	G, T	Mature stem, good colour seeds, before fully ripe
Rumex obtusifolius	Dock (field)	F, S	G, T	Flowers mature good colour red/brown seeds, well before dispersement
Salvia officinalis	Sage	F, S	A	Full purple flower, or after flower for seed pod stage
Santolina chamaecyparissus	Lavender cotton	F	A	At yellow flower ball stage
Scabiosa hybrid	Paper moon scabious	S	A	Seed head 'parachute' ball fully formed, before natural die back
Secale cereale	Rye (field)	S	A	Mature green heads, or later as green going yellow before seeds shed naturally
Sedum spp	Stonecrop	S	A	After flowering, when leaves start to drop from stem, and mauve/red colour of head still evident
Silene spp	Campion (red/white)	S	A	Pod mature green, going brown, before seed shatter
Sinapis alba	White mustard	S	A	Green seed stage
Sisyrinchium striatum	Satin flower	S	A	Flowering stems turn from green to brown, at seed dispersement
Solidago canadensis	Golden rod	F	A	Mid to prime bloom
Sparganium erectum	Blanched bur reed	F, S	A	At full flowering
Spiraea × billiardii 'Trimphans'	Spiraea	F, S	A	Mid bloom, or just mature; quick dry to hold pink colour
Stachys tanata	Lamb's tongue	S	A	Brown seed stage
Tagetes erecta	French marigold	F, S	A	In mid to full bloom, or green seed head stage
Tanacetum vulgare	Tansy	F, S	A	Mid to full bloom before yellow fades to ocre, or later when brown head
Tripleurospermum maritimum	Mayweed	S, F	A	Past bloom, pluck out faded petals, keep yellow centres
Triticum aestirum	Wheat (field)	S	A	Green milk ear stage, as green/yellow, and golden before corns drop
Typha latifolia	Great reed mace	F, S	A	Best when small portion of stem top still protrudes above brown swelling
Various ferns spp	Ferns (woodland)	L	A, P	Mature green at growing tip, before spores set on underside
Veronica longifolia/spicata	Speedwell	F, S	A	In mid flower, and after flowering as spikes turn good brown
Xeranthemum abbum	Everlasting Flower	F	A	Mid to perfect bloom
Zea mays	Corn on the cob (maize)	S	A	After tassel, at harvest of mature cobs, with pale green going gold husks